MILLION DOLLAR OUTLINES

MILLION DOLLAR OUTLINES

David Farland

WordFire Press
Colorado Springs, Colorado

ISBN: 978-1-61475-176-2

Cover images by Shutterstock

Cover design by Kevin J. Anderson

Book Design by RuneWright, LLC
www.RuneWright.com

Published by
WordFire Press, an imprint of
WordFire, Inc.
PO Box 1840
Monument CO 80132

Kevin J. Anderson & Rebecca Moesta Publishers

WordFire Press Trade Paperback Edition 2014
Printed in the USA
wordfirepress.com

THE MILLION DOLLAR WRITING SERIES

When seeking advice, always consider the source. Many self-appointed "experts" write how-to books without themselves ever accomplishing the thing they are trying to teach you how to do.

In the Million Dollar Writing Series, each of our authors has sold a minimum of one million dollars of commercial product in their field. They have proved themselves, and here they share their wisdom, advice, and experience with you.

There are many factors in becoming a successful writer, and we cannot guarantee that you'll break into the top levels, but we hope you find the advice to be useful and enlightening.

TABLE OF CONTENTS

FOREWORD

David Farland has trained dozens of *New York Times* bestselling authors over the years—people like Stephenie Meyer (*Twilight*), Brandon Sanderson (*Wheel of Time*), and Brandon Mull (*Fablehaven*) all came to him before they had ever sold a novel, then went on to make millions.

As a greenlighting analyst, David Farland worked helping with novels and films (as a consultant he urged Scholastic to push *Harry Potter* big, long before they were willing to do so).

And as a videogame designer he helped create stellar games like *Starcraft: Brood War*.

Eventually, people began asking him to teach a class on how to integrate high-level audience analysis into the design of a new intellectual property—a book or movie—and his popular writing course "Million-Dollar Outlines" was born.

This book is used during the course as a reference, a refresher for many of the main ideas. An earlier edition was hastily thrown together. This new edition is heavily rewritten, and hopefully will help you learn not just how to outline, but how to begin tweaking your work in major intellectual properties before you ever begin writing.

OVERVIEW

What Kind of Writer Are You?

Let's face it: there are a lot of places where you can learn to outline a story. I've read books on the topic, studied card systems used in Hollywood, and even computer programs that can all teach you how to outline well.

In fact, I bought a program recently for $70 that did a pretty decent job of teaching you how to create a good working outline—but only if you wanted to write a "hero journey" story. It wasn't much help in writing romances or comedies or several other types of tales.

So this book can help you to outline any story, but more importantly it also seeks to explain to you why some story ideas are better than others. Why do some ideas electrify wide audiences while others leave readers scratching their collective heads? How can you tell the difference so that you don't waste your time writing a book or screenplay that has an audience of just one?

To understand this, I need to get into the basic psychology of storytelling, taking you much deeper than your average "how to" manual or software does.

This requires that you first learn what constitutes a potential bestseller, recognize the qualities of a good story, and then learn how to outline it in such a way as to bring out the best in it.

So, long before we ever talk about outlining, we're going to spend dozens of pages on audience analysis and story theory.

You may be wondering if this book is for you. I'll be honest: maybe it isn't. Read the next page to find out why.

Two Approaches to Storytelling

There are two major approaches for writing a story: discovery writing and outlining. Neither approach is completely right nor wrong, and most authors take a hybrid approach. So let's discuss each approach, along with its strengths and pitfalls.

Discovery Writers

A discovery writer is one who likes to begin a story without really knowing where it will end. Stephen King is an excellent example of a discovery writer. Such writers enjoy the process of "discovering" the story as it unfolds. Often, a writer who is deeply involved in a novel will be writing about a character and suddenly recognize that unexpected things are happening: the killer in a mystery turns out to be the protagonist himself, or the hero actually fails in his quest.

Discovery writing is an excellent way to create stories that feel organic. Characters often tend to come out well-rounded in discovery stories, and settings come to life.

However, I've known countless discovery writers who have problems with weak middles and sluggish endings because they didn't control where the story was going; or maybe the writer may take ages to write a novel because they end up following characters down blind alleys.

Very often, in discovery novels the focus on the primary character's shifts from one protagonist to another over the course of the novel, or the major conflicts that the author started with aren't the ones that get resolved. When this happens, the reader feels cheated because the author hasn't kept the promises that were set up at the beginning of the tale.

Yet many authors find that extra enjoyment in taking this approach because the story always feels fresh, vital, and alive. It makes the crafting of the tale fun, in and of itself, so that regardless of whether the piece sells, the work is enjoyable. So if you love the process of crafting the tale, this might be your favorite mode of writing.

Just remember that not all projects can be written through the discovery method. I've created a number of novels for major franchises like *Star Wars* and *The Mummy*. Some of them have earned hundreds of thousands of dollars. But franchise owners will insist on a beautiful outline before they greenlight a project.

If you are solidly in the camp of discovery writers, if you never want to learn to work in others' franchises, then this book may be of no help to you at all. In working with writers, I find that about ten percent of them fit into this category. You probably know who you are: you may be the kind of writer who likes to write what are called "small" stories, intimate tales based upon your own past, your own personal life. Or like Stephen King, maybe you just enjoy the process of discovery so much that it becomes your primary drive for writing. It becomes addictive.

If this describes you, don't waste your time and money on this book.

Outline Writers

Outlining writers enjoy creating a story by considering how to develop an engrossing tale, told at a great pace, with jaw-dropping plot twists. For them, plot is often paramount. There are plenty of plotting writers on the bestseller lists—people like Kevin J. Anderson or Ken Follett. For outliners, the fun of writing often comes in the pre-writing phase, where they sit and think, "Wouldn't it be cool if…?"

The strengths of outlining are that numerous. It is often both easier and faster to draft a book or screenplay based upon an outline because you know exactly where the story is going. There are fewer pitfalls and temptations to rewrite, since you're not following characters down blind alleys. Writing from an outline makes the author more productive.

Sometimes, big stories can be sold on the basis of an outline alone, so that the writer can get paid for doing his work well in advance. A "proven" writer can make deals for millions of dollars based upon an exciting outline.

The weakness of outlining is that for some authors the process of writing that first draft can begin to feel mechanical—as if it is too much like a regular day job. As a critic, I find that stories written from outlines can feel a bit "thin," as if the characters and scenes exist only to forward the plot. So as a writer, you need to guard against that.

In other cases, the author is so excited to get the plot down on paper, that the prose itself is deficit. The character voices may be weak and unformed, the sentence structures hastily written and inelegant. In other words, the author is so excited about getting something on paper that he doesn't give proper consideration as to his tale.

One other weakness of outlining is that once the outline is complete, the author may feel that the story has already been invented, and he no longer needs to write it. One writer in Hollywood was known for creating great plots, which he would tell his friends in bars or at dinner parties. But after he had perfected his tale through three or four tellings, he no longer felt the need to write it all—and thus would ignore it forever. He'd lost the excitement. His friends were always amazed at the number of great movies he created—none of which ever made it to a first draft.

But there are ways to combine the advantages of both approaches to writing....

Taking a Middle Ground

Many authors will take a hybrid approach to writing, using some outlining methods but leaving themselves open to free-write.

For example, you might find that you can outline just the world for your story. Whether you set your tale in a fantasy world, or in twelfth century Germany, or in a far-future dystopia, the world is not likely to change. Yet your characters and societies and their resulting conflicts will all grow out of that world. So you can develop a wonderfully detailed milieu, with wars and major conflicts and maps and notes on various subcultures and political rivalries and religions—and even have a strong idea of where your story is going—yet you may choose to "discover" who your characters are. Or maybe as you sit and think about how to best describe that world, you'll create elaborate set pieces of description, bringing your world to a life more deeply than you anticipated, making new discoveries about it.

In short, you may outline much of the tale, but leave some parts to discover. Tolkien seemed to work this way, creating Middle Earth and some of his characters long before he wrote *Lord of the Rings*.

I personally will often outline a novel in thirds—so that I know where I'm going with opening scenes, but then stop partway through to consider how to handle the next stage of a tale. I know from long experience that by the time that I reach the middle of my novel, I will have changed emphasis and direction often enough so that I will need to "discover" what happens next. I almost never give my "themes" any thought before I begin, and so I often discover the theme of my tales, and the controlling metaphors as a I write. All of which means that I don't quite know how it will all end—not really.

In any case, any one of these approaches—discovery writing, outlining, or a hybrid approach—can work beautifully for a professional writer.

You as an author may need to discover through trial and error which technique you enjoy most.

So this book will teach you how to outline in an effort to increase your productivity and the value of your finished product, as well as to discover new revenue streams. More importantly, it strikes at how to recognize and develop those great ideas that form the core of a blockbuster intellectual property.

HOW THIS MANUAL
IS ORGANIZED

The process of inventing a novel doesn't all occur in one neat little step.

Before you can outline a story, you need to "brainstorm" it. The brainstorming process is a creative one—a right-brain function that comes often over weeks and months as you think about what you'd like to write. You'll get a flash of a scene that appears in your mind, like the piece to a jigsaw puzzle. Later you might come up with an intriguing idea for a character, or maybe a plot twist, and each of those are pieces to the puzzle, too.

Not all of the pieces that you find fit together neatly. It's like that crate full of puzzles that my mother used to keep—with dozens of old puzzles all thrown together.

But eventually you find some that fit, and others you craft from scratch, and you begin putting each of these pieces together into a coherent story.

These images and twists and characters and events are the meat of your plot, and coming up with them may take weeks or months. In fact, you'll keep getting new ideas as you write your novel or screenplay, and perhaps even long after. For example, twenty years ago I wrote a two-novel series with the books *Serpent Catch* and *Path of the Hero*. Last summer I woke up one night and realized that "If I just added this scene, it would really smooth out the transition between those novels."

Of course, no one rewrites novels after twenty years. We have to get the book onto the shelves. The same is true with movies. There is a saying in Hollywood: "Movies are never finished, just abandoned." Most filmmakers are editing their movie right up to within a day or two of its distribution.

So creating a strong outline is a process that often starts out strong, but really can take time. Revision of your story, even in outline form, is an important part of the creative process. A few years ago I was talking to Frank Frazetta, one of the greatest fantasy illustrators of all time. I was gazing at some of his paintings and noticed that they had changed subtly since they had been first published in the 1970s.I asked him about it, and he said, "Oh, yes, I take them out every few months and work on them. I might put a new wash over sections to deepen and bring out the color, or I might add a few highlights or new details." After thirty years, he was still creating his paintings.

You'll have the same urge to continue working on your outline, too. Try not to take too long in this process.

As you write the first draft, you'll normally recognizes weaknesses in your outline and correct them then. Don't drag out the process for years.

But before you start your work, you need to get some basic ideas of what the shape of your story might be, who your characters are, what settings you want to describe, and so on.

While creating a story is a right-brain process, the act of outlining it in a logical fashion takes place in the left hemisphere of the brain.

Your goal then is to generate enough information in the creative half of your brain so that the logical portion of your mind can study the tale, recognize weaknesses, and make it strong enough to become a bestseller.

So our organization follows certain steps.

Step 1: Identify what Elements make a Bestseller.

In the first section of this course, we'll look at storytelling from a theoretical point of view, to try to understand how to tell stories that will please a wide audience. We'll also study bestselling movies and books and find the characteristics that are common to bestsellers.

Step 2: Identify the Elements that Let You Plot a Story.

Most books and computer programs on plotting give you a general idea of how plots work. But in this book we get into much more detail. We don't just study overall story shape or how to create character arcs, we get into how plotting devices can be used to bolster any plot and make your story more interesting.

Step 3: Plot.

As you study step one and two, you will undoubtedly get more and more ideas about how to handle your own story. The puzzle pieces will begin to fit together. You'll think about the basic shape and form of your story. You'll consider how to develop try/fail cycles, and how you might use various plotting devices to strengthen the tale. So in this third step, we get into the thick of it and develop an outline.

This first draft of an outline begs to be perfected, deepened and made more poignant, so you may take time to workshop it with other writers and revise it accordingly.

Once you finish the outline, you can turn it into a novel or a screenplay, or develop the story for a video game or television series.

In short, the outline is a roadmap for creating a large intellectual property.

SECTION 1

WHAT MAKES A BESTSELLING STORY?

This section gives you important background information that will help you think about and shape your story. We examine questions like, "Why People Read?" "Defining a Million-Dollar Property," and Audience Analysis for books, movies, and television.

INTRODUCTION: WRITING AS A FORM OF ENTERTAINMENT

You want to be a writer. That's great. But how well do your desires fulfill an audience's desires? Will the audience accept you?

The average person who takes up writing may do so for a variety of reasons. Very often writers are passionate people who feel the need for self-expression more deeply than others. For them writing, like music or painting, offers an outlet where they can engage in heightened communication, expressing emotion as powerfully as possible.

Some are revolutionaries, out to change the world.

Other writers are less passionate in general, but may have a specific conflict in life that they need to express. For example I've known writers who have suffered from child abuse, spouse abuse, or unusual sexual desires and who need to create fictionalized stories about it as a form of therapy.

Again, I know writers who have no specific passion or conflict, but who write merely to attract attention. They see the medium as a road to fame and fortune.

The fact is that your motivations for wanting to write are probably complex. You may have a few great passions, you may want to be rich and famous, you may need therapy.

In fact, your reasons might be primarily economical. You may recognize that being a writer gives you a certain kind of independence from local economies so that you can live in an area where good jobs are tough to find.

Heck, I've known many writers who take it up for health reasons. When I started, I was so sick that I couldn't hold down a regular job.

Whatever your reasons for wanting to be a writer, the audience doesn't give a damn.

Audience members each have their own agenda. And in order to satisfy them, in order to sell widely so that you can make a living from your art, you need to understand your audience.

So, Why do People Seek out Stories?

The answer to that question depends on who you ask. Many people will tell you that they read or go to movies for "entertainment," which is a vague and unsatisfactory answer. After all, one man imagines himself laughing when he's entertained while the wife standing next to him imagines herself crying.

So the answer to the question is quite complex, and the reasons for seeking stories aren't necessarily the same for all readers.

For example I don't read horror. I've seen enough real horrors in life that the fictions I have read seldom can even faze me. Nor do I like murder mysteries. I had friends murdered by a serial killer when I was a child (they were hacked into pieces and thrown from a speeding car). So such tales may be too painful to read.

Nor do I consider myself to be an expert on romance. But I will talk about some attractions that are common to almost all fiction, and I'll discuss how to use that knowledge. Before that, I'd like you to perform an exercise.

Exercise

You probably have a good idea about what you want to write—horror, mainstream, fantasy, historical, romance, westerns, religious fiction, and whatnot. Sit down for ten minutes and list five things that you feel you most like in the fiction you read. Then list the biggest potential danger you see in trying to create that effect.

Doing this exercise will help you understand who your potential audience is, and some of the challenges you may face in reaching that audience.

For example, let's say you like fantasy. Your response may resemble the following:

1—I like to escape to strange new worlds

But I'm afraid that the worlds I create might not be strange enough. I sometimes wonder if I have enough imagination to compete with the likes of Tolkien. Other times I imagine things that are so alien that I'm not sure I can communicate them to my audience.

WHAT IS ENTERTAINMENT?

Why do people read for recreation instead of doing something else? Why not go skiing, watch a movie, play chess, or hang out on Hollywood Boulevard?

Why do We Crave Stories?

I've never seen a definition that encompasses all types of entertainment, and there are many forms—sports, listening to music, attending parties, watching movies. When I was a prison guard, I knew killers who killed for pleasure, women who tried to seduce men for enjoyment. What do these have in common with fiction?

We have to answer that question before we can move on.

Years ago when I first began asking myself why people read, I really felt that the answers didn't mesh.

Professors in college said that we read for escape, or because we enjoy the beautiful sounds of words, or for insights.

Fine, I thought, but I can escape by getting out of the house. If I want beautiful sounds, I'll listen to Dan Fogelberg. If I'm looking to understand the world, I might be better off reading the encyclopedia or a newspaper.

Why do People Crave Stories, Good Stories, Written Down?

One clue came to me almost by accident. I happened to meet a professor who was talking to a friend. The professor was one of my favorite writing instructors, a woman who vehemently forbade her students from writing trashy genre fiction—romance, science fiction, fantasy, horror, westerns or anything of that ilk. She discouraged her students from even reading it, fearing that it would subvert their higher impulses as artists.

So imagine my astonishment when I heard her discussing with another professor how she had wept the previous night after reading a trashy romance novel. I was flabbergasted to discover this ... this deceit. Why, she was nothing but a hypocrite!

So I confronted her, asking why she would even bother to read a romance novel. She explained that she read romance to relax. When life got stressful, her job got hectic, it was a good way to unwind.

Indeed, once I began asking others why they read, the words "stressful" and "relaxing" began to crop up more and more.

But on the face of it, that answer seemed absurd! When we read, we take part in a common dream. We vicariously experience what is happening. People go through tremendous difficulties in a novel. People get run over by cars or stalked by serial killers. People get raped, beaten, sold as slaves and struggle through constant turmoil. And it isn't happening to others—it's happening to us, as readers.

Books aren't relaxing at all, are they?

And that's when I saw a possible answer.

In an early writing class, one instructor talked about Feralt's triangle. Feralt was French writer who studied what made successful stories. He said that in a successful story, the tale begins with a character that has a problem. As we read, the suspense rises, the problems become more complex and have more far-reaching consequences, until we reach the climax of the story, where the hero's fortune changes. Afterward, the problem is resolved, the tension diminishes, and the reader is allowed to return to a relaxed state.

He put it on paper like this:

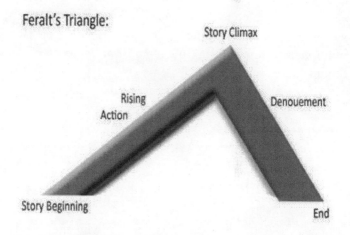

His vision wasn't new or astonishing. After all, his work was based on the writings of Aristotle. (Note that most experts credit Freytag with developing the plot triangle. My teacher wasn't one of them.)

But shortly after my experience with my closet romance-reading professor, I came upon an article in a medical journal and suddenly found myself looking at a chart remarkably similar to the plot triangle. The confluence of the three ideas helped me strike to the core of just exactly why people read for recreation.

The article explained some recent experiments on endorphins—internally created opiates that our body uses to help control pain. You see, as we live through our daily lives, we constantly are faced with minor pains. Cells age and die, we get minor cuts and abrasions, and to fight the pain that comes with these cellular deaths, our body creates a certain low level of endorphins. In essence, our body is constantly drugging us. If not, we would literally feel ourselves dying, wasting away, from moment to moment.

However, when you get injured—when you get cut or stick your hand in a vat of acid—cells die on a massive level and your brain suddenly registers the pain. This of course serves as a warning to get away from the source of pain—the vat of acid, the scalding hot chocolate, or whatever. But the brain also begins creating more endorphins in an effort to diminish the pain.

Eventually, the level of opiates produced by the body matches the level of damage involved, and then the pain you experience diminishes or vanishes completely. Depending on the severity of your injury, the process can take hours or days. A small cut may stop hurting in hours; a severe burn might not quit aching for weeks.

This is all a very common process in the body. It's called a "biofeedback loop," and the body uses it in thousands of ways. For example, as your body recognizes sugar in the bloodstream, it signals to the pancreas to begin secreting insulin so that you can metabolize the sugar. When the amount of sugar in your blood drops, the pancreas is then allowed to stop producing insulin.

In another example, as your brain recognizes a lack of oxygen in your bloodstream, it sends an impulse to your lungs to breathe more deeply. Once the bloodstream is oxygenated, your lungs are allowed to go back to rest.

Our body works based upon thousands of different kinds of biofeedback loops.

The interesting thing about endorphin levels to me was this: everyone has a resting level of endorphins in their bloodstream, and based on this level, we each have our own threshold of pain. Thus, if you jab me with a pin to a certain depth, I will recognize pain at a very consistent level.

But what happens when I get injured, say severely cut, and my body raises the level of endorphins?

The answer is: I will feel less background pain. The pinprick that hurt me a day before may go unnoticed the next, simply because I am naturally sedated.

This is why runners, people who walk barefoot, or people who subject themselves to rigorous and painful exercises have a much higher tolerance for pain than those who do not.

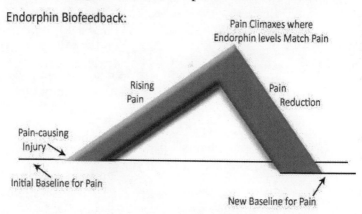

Endorphin Biofeedback:

As I say, biofeedback loops are everywhere in the body, and I studied them often back when I was in pre-med.

But what fascinated me about this chart was how similar it looked to the plot triangle, and how similar the idea of coping with stress was with the concept of coping with pain.

Think of it, the body has to have some way to cope with stress. Otherwise, we'd get more and more stressed out until we all went nuts.

At that point I recognized that reading a formed story that conforms to Feralt's plotting outline might be a type of emotional exercise that allows us to handle stress.

Obviously, each of us has background stress in our lives. Your stress may come from problems in your marriage, or fear that you'll lose your job. It may have to do with concerns for your health, or the health of a friend. It may have to do with deadlines or other time pressures. Right now, without thinking much, you can probably come up with a dozen stress-inducing problems that you have to deal with today.

To cope with life's little problems, we have three options:

—We may *remove* the source of stress completely. If you're out of money, you can make a lot more, until you're no longer stressed. If you're sick, you can get cured. But removing the source of your stress isn't always attainable. Sometimes you have to try something else.

—We may *escape* from stress by taking a vacation perhaps, or a night on the town. This is a temporary attempt to resolve the stress, but it doesn't always help. Have you ever spent a vacation where you just agonized about what you needed to do at work? We can't spend our lives at Disneyland.

—We can perform emotional *exercise* to help cope with the stress. In this scenario, you're like a weightlifter, doing your reps in order to strengthen yourself. This is what happens when we entertain ourselves with reading, watching movies, watching sports, go skydiving, or try to "entertain" ourselves in any of hundreds of other ways.

The fascinating thing about a story is that it lets you escape from your stress and exercise simultaneously. By reading a book or watching a movie, to a degree you escape from your own life, your own world, and become immersed in a fictive universe. You take an emotional vacation from your own world. Typically this is most true in the opening of a story, where the author spends a good deal of time establishing the setting and the conflicts may be less significant and may appear more easily resolvable than at the end.

But if a tale merely distracts you, if it relates dull incidents about characters that never face significant trials, in the end you will feel cheated. You may say, "That story was good, but it would have been better if ..."

Merely distracting a reader isn't satisfying enough. If it were, people would read travelogues instead of stories.

No, in order for a story to be really satisfying, it must also be rejuvenating. When you read you must enter a world where you are placed in meaningful conflict, conflicts that build and deepen and grow. In other words, we exercise by dealing with imaginary conflicts.

In short, as many other authors have noted, the situations that are intolerable to you in real life are those that you crave in fiction.

For example, only a madman would want to leave his home, his family, and his friends, get stalked by the nine Black Riders, take a sword blade to the chest, battle orcs in the mines of Moria, nearly starve to death on the road, and confront Sauron in Mordor.

All of those things would be intolerable in real life.

But we crave them in fiction. Here's why: Your subconscious mind does not completely recognize the difference between your real experiences and those that occur only in the imagination. So, when you become Frodo Baggins walking the road to the Crack of Doom, chased by

Black Riders, the subconscious mind responds to some degree as if it were really happening. When you are Robin Hood, grieving for your dead father, your mind reacts as if it were really happening to you.

Indeed, the more completely you become immersed in a fictive tale, the more totally your body will respond.

How often have you found yourself reading a book with your heart hammering so badly that you had to stop? How often have you found sweat on your brow and your breathing shallow? So the body responds. It says, "I thought life was bad at the office, but this stress is killing me! Let's handle it."

In short, as your body gets stressed it releases chemicals to help you cope with the stress. Adrenaline and cortisol make your heart pound, your senses sharpen, and force your body to begin to store energy as fat.

At that point, some biofeedback mechanism kicks in. Your body, in an effort to handle the imaginary stress, seeks some way to cope.

As you seek for answers to the problems, your body releases dopamine in small amounts, exactly the way that a dog gets dopamine as a reward for sniffing at the trail of a rabbit. In short, you get little bursts of satisfaction, even as the conflicts deepen.

When your reach the climax to the novel, when you're standing at the Crack of Doom, you reach the most important of your emotional exercise. Your heart may be pounding furiously, and in desperation you search for a release from stress.

When the stress is resolved and the obstacles overcome, just as the cortisol and adrenaline stop pumping, your body gives you another reward: it floods your bloodstream with serotonin, and when that happens, I suspect that the biofeedback loop is completed. Instead of suffering stress, your brains says, "Great job, you solved the problem. Here's a surfeit of serotonin as your reward," and you begin to bask in happy, fuzzy enjoyment.

You sit back in your chair and sigh, and say, "Wow, what a relief! I feel so much better!"

And the truth is you do feel better.

You've just performed an emotional exercise, very similar to a physical exercise. Reading is to the mind as aerobics is to the heart and lungs. Because you have performed this emotional exercise, you will be better able to handle the little stresses in your day-to-day life. The minor problems at the office seem to diminish in intensity and even the major catastrophes aren't so intimidating.

In short, all forms of recreation boil down to this: recreation is any activity that helps us cope with stress by putting ourselves at risk in some controlled way so as to artificially raise stress for a short period of time

Let me show you how reading relates to most other forms of recreation: in some forms of entertainment, we may put our very lives in jeopardy—such as when we are skydiving, mountain climbing, bungee jumping, auto racing, and so on. But in order for us as participants to be rejuvenated by an experience, we must be able to control the element of danger. For example, jumping from an airplane without a parachute is suicide. But jumping from an airplane with a parachute is recreation. For me, racing a car at 600 mph would be suicide, but I'd feel fairly comfortable driving 140 mph, because I would be able to control the vehicle. I once heard a cowboy say that he "liked a little target practice from time to time, but that didn't mean that he wanted to engage in a shootout every time he went to the bank."

The sense of being in control of the danger is vital to the value of the exercise in rejuvenation.

When we play a game of skill—such as chess or golf— we don't put ourselves in physical danger, but we do put our own status on the line. We put our place in society, our reputation, in jeopardy. This is particularly true in upper-level tournament sports. So when we play sports, we still have the elements of placing ourselves in jeopardy in a controlled environment.

If there is no jeopardy, the sport is unrewarding. For example, playing golf with a six-year old would be a bore. I could probably crush most six year olds. But playing Tiger Woods would be just as unrewarding—I don't have the skills to even try. But trying to beat my best friend—and thereby either slightly raising or lowering my status in his eyes—could be entertaining.

In many sports we don't risk our health or reputation— instead we may risk our wealth. Poker, dog racing, and many other games are valuable as recreation simply because we invest money into them. In short, we place ourselves in economic jeopardy. The more money we risk, the bigger the thrill. If we bet too much, the threat becomes unbearable. If we bet too little, it's not really interesting.

Do you see the relationship between reading and other forms of recreation? Here it is: when we read, we buy into a shared dream, a shared fiction, and by doing so we put ourselves in emotional jeopardy.

To some degree, we thrust ourselves into the hands of a storyteller, trusting that he will deliver us safely from a daydream that swiftly turns into a nightmare. But we don't want to trust him too much.

If the emotional jeopardy is too small, we get bored.

If the emotional jeopardy is too great, we'll close the book.

If the author abuses our trust—if for example he doesn't end the story, but leaves us instead in greater emotional jeopardy, or if the ending is too ambiguous, we will no longer trust the author and we'll shun his fiction.

This same need for a happy outcome is true in other forms of recreation. Have you ever noticed that when your team is winning regularly, the stands at the football or basketball stadium rapidly fill up? We don't want to invest emotional energy in a team that will let us down. We don't want to watch games that our team can't win. We won't gamble on the lottery if no one ever hits the jackpot.

So here is the secret that I couldn't learn in college: reading for recreation generally works best only as we read well-formed stories—tales where there is an ascending level of stress, doubt as to the outcome, followed by a conclusion where the stress is relieved.

In short, those "trashy" genre stories that my writing teachers didn't want me to read—the romances, fantasy, westerns, and so on—sell well precisely because the audience does know within certain parameters how the story will end.

At the very heart of it, reading stories or viewing them allows us to perform an emotional exercise. And the better you as a writer are at creating fiction that meets your audience's deepest needs, the better your work will sell.

In later chapters I talk about what a story is—a setup, expanding try/fail cycles, a climax and resolution. But form follows function. Just as we create chairs—whether they be stools, thrones, or lazy-boy recliners—to fit some basic human needs, a stories are also shaped to fit human needs.

Now, many types of writing aren't stories. You can write anecdotes, interesting accounts of things that have happened to people. You can write essays to convince me of your philosophies. You can write a slice of life, or tell me a joke. But each of those types of writing is as different in form as an elephant is from a duck.

So, when we as professional genre writers talk about what a story is, we are talking about the form that has been dis-covered through trial and error by writers over the centuries.

This understanding of what a story is, and why and how it functions, leads me to conclude that there are a few basic principles to writing a formed story, as discussed below:

—*A Writer's Job is to Guide the Reader through a Stress Exercise.* As an author I write fiction because I recognize that I am performing a service to my readers. They are looking for an emotional exercise, and it is my job to deliver. If I write unformed fiction—stories that have no ends, stories that are ambiguous in the end, or stories that have displeasing ends—I'm not fulfilling the trust that readers place in me. I'm not doing the job that they're paying me for. In such a case, I will rightfully lose my readership.

—*All Stories Must Create a Balance of Stress.* If I do not create enough stress in my story, the story will bore the reader. If I create too much stress, the story will become unbearable and the reader will put it down. My job is to create a pleasing level of stress that rises toward a dramatic climax, then resolves.

—*Not All Readers Will Be Pleased by the Same Story.* Different readers require different levels of stress. Some people crave horror, just as some crave the adrenaline rush of sky diving. I don't like either activity. At the same time, things that would bore me—say the story of a boy who wonders if he'll ever get his first car—may be perfectly suited to a person who craves a less-rigorous emotional exercise. Thus, I will never write a story that will perfectly please all readers.

—*Stress Levels Need to be Carefully Controlled Throughout the Story.* In order to hold my reader, I must create some stress. At the same time, in order to make the story feel safe enough so that my reader gets emotionally involved, I have to make that stress level "safe." I can do this in one of several ways. Typically, I make the conflict feel safer by transporting my reader into another time, place, or persona, but I can also relieve stress by offering hope to my readers that the stress will be resolved.

—*I Must De-stress My Reader Properly.* This typically means that I will resolve all of the important conflicts created in the story, usually in the most powerful way possible. My characters need to be more than relieved, they need to be almost giddy. Most of the time, I need to release my reader into a setting that is serene and at rest.

WHAT IS A STORY, AND HOW DOES IT WORK?

Can you define the term *story*?

You've seen thousands of them on television and the movies. You've probably heard them from the time that you were a toddler on your mother's lap, and you may hear more of them while standing in line at a water cooler at work.

In fact, you've seen so many of them that you recognize them without thinking about their integral parts. They're like ants that way. You spot a bug on the ground down at your feet, plodding along with a bit of a leaf, and you go "Ah, an ant!" But you don't have to fall down on your face and peer at it, count its legs and antennae, and ponder for long in order to recognize that this is indeed an ant and not some other vermin with a similar exoskeleton. You know instantly that it's an ant, not a beetle posing as one.

You've seen and heard so many stories that, in fact, that you don't just recognize them, you subconsciously judge them.

As you're watching a movie, you evaluate how the story stacks up to all others. If you feel something amiss, you might even begin to critique it consciously. "Ah," you might tell yourself, "this just doesn't work as a romance. The male lead is too creepy. I really want the girl to run away from him, not fall into his arms."

If, in the end, the writer fails to even create a story, you'll know. You might say, "The hero saved the girl way too easily," or "I just didn't feel anything at the end."

So you know a story when you see it.

But what makes a story? What makes a great tale powerful? Why do we care about stories? Why do people want to read them instead of play videogames?

The answers to these questions aren't easy to come by. Many people have tried to define what makes a story—Aristotle, Feralt, Emerson, Budrys, and dozens of others.

The Scope of the Problem

Most people who try to define what a story is are secretly more interested in another question: what makes a great story powerful?

Thus, Aristotle began to define a story in those terms. He reasoned that a great story has a sympathetic hero with a powerful conflict, and as the story progresses, it has a "rising action" which arouses passion in the viewer until the problem is resolved and we either feel elation that the hero has won, or we pity his fallen state.

Feralt's Triangle

Feralt said that in a successful story, the tale begins with a character in a relaxed state, but soon a problem is introduced. As we progress through the tale, the suspense rises, the problem becomes more complex and has more far-reaching consequences, until we reach the climax of the story, where the hero's fortune changes—either he resolved the problem, is destroyed, or must learn to live with the problem. In any case, the tension diminishes, and the reader is allowed to return to a relaxed state.

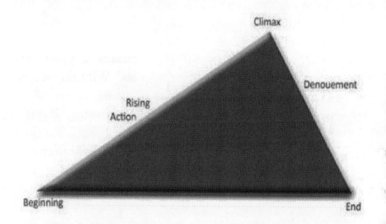

That triangle describes most commercial fiction of the 1800s, and indeed describes most of the genre fiction, television, and movies today.

But then the 1900s came along, and a number of authors began to reject "formed" fiction. In part they were reacting to the fact that so many of the genres had reached a point where plots had become so rigid that the outcomes of the stories were predictable.

In short, they were looking for new and exciting ways to form stories. In some cases, authors began to write non-formed fiction altogether. Some writers, the social Darwinists, even reached the conclusion that "since there is no god, and life itself is just a random series of events, it makes no sense to try to make sense of life through our fiction. Thus, to create a formed story, one that seeks to reach some kind of logical conclusion, is in fact to perpetuate a lie."

So in the early 1900s we began to get the "slice of life" stories and vignettes by such fine writers as Virginia Wolfe. The point wasn't to tell a formed story, but simply to capture a fascinating moment in a character's life—perhaps a conversation, or a spring day.

Other writers recognized that readers had developed such a solid sense of story that the reader often filled in the gaps himself when reading. In short, there is a subconscious collaboration between the author and the audience. Thus, Ernest Hemingway wrote a story once and sent it to his agent. He penned a note with it that said, "I wrote a story about a man who receives a telegram telling him that his son has died in the war. Then he goes to a bar and gets drunk. Afterward, he goes home and hangs himself. But I cut off the beginning and the end. I think that the one scene is enough—they'll get the rest from the tone." His short story, "A Clean, Well-lighted Place," is one of Hemingway's most celebrated, and can be found in a number of short story collections.

With some people rejecting form completely and other writers truncating their stories and purposely omitting parts of the tale—the ending in particular—or otherwise making the tale obscure, it soon became difficult for a critic to define what a story is.

After all, if we define it too rigidly, we take the risk that new authors will become slavish in their imitations of past works, and thus will not experiment with new forms.

Given this, some critics of the 1940s and beyond will glibly tell you, "A story is anything that the author says that it is." But such a broad description merely infuriates a new writer who can't figure out why his plot doesn't seem to be working.

So, let's take the bones of a story and see if we can figure out just when it becomes a story in form. Let's take a true piece of trivia:

In the town where I grew up, there lived a man who kept three pet lions in his house—until they ate him.

By the broadest definition of what a story is, that's a story. It's written on paper, I'm a *New York Times* bestselling author, and if I say it's a story, it's a story.

But you as the reader of course recognize that it isn't a story. It has too many gaping holes. "Really?" you might ask. "Did this really happen? Why would anyone keep lions in their house? Where did this happen and when? Why did the lions eat him? What really happened?"

So let's try a longer version:

In the town that I lived, Monroe, Oregon, we had a man who kept three lions in his house. This was back in 1979. My father owned a meat company, and every day or two the man, Paul, would load his pet lions into the back of his pickup and bring them to our store.

He would buy steaks, beef bones, and bags of dog food to feed to his lions. I actually went out and petted them on several occasions, and the sight of them always thrilled the out-of-town customers.

Paul was quite wealthy. He built a huge house with a sunken living room, and catwalks along the upper levels gave his lions a nice place to perch while he sat on his bean bags and watched television.

In fact, he bought the lions from a good friend of mine, a fellow named Jack Lawrence, who sold exotic pets. Jack used to keep an ostrich in his house in a bird cage, and he always had a couple of Bengal tigers out in his barns, along with lions and bears, and huge white buffalo. It turns out that not many people want lions, and so you could buy one back then for about five hundred dollars.

Then Paul's lions ate him.

So we've got a longer version. You might see that in this one, I've answered some objections. I gave you more of a setting—a time and place—and I even went so far as to let you know where the lions came from, thus making the tale more plausible.

But this isn't a story yet, is it? At the best, it's merely an incident or an event.

Ronald Tobias's book, *20 Master Plots*, contains a good discussion of story as told from the point of view of a mainstream scholar. He comes close to getting a definition, and reaches the conclusion that a story is "a series of causally related events."

He reaches his conclusion thus: Somerset Maugham once said that unrelated events were not a story, but causally related events were. Maugham provided the example: "The king died, and then the queen died."

Those are mere occurrences, not a story. We get no satisfaction from them. Indeed, we don't really care.

But imagine if you said, "The king died, and then the queen died of grief."

Maugham suggested that that was a story, and Tobias agrees. The causal relationship creates something of a story. It has a beginning, implies a middle, and it ends. The tale answers the question "Why?"

But it's not really a story, is it? If it were, our jobs would be so much easier. Here's a short story written by his definition: The chicken crossed the road, got hungry from its journey, and caught a caterpillar to eat!

Obviously, that doesn't stack up well against *Hamlet*, or even *Harry Potter*.

The caterpillar story will never sell, nor will the queen's death. The problem is that Tobias hasn't paid attention to what stories do: they simultaneously try to make sense of the world and entertain. His example makes sense of the world, but does not entertain. He has only a part of the equation.

Here is a little better definition: a story is a series of causally related events and actions *that are meant to entertain* and that answer an important question: "Why?"

You see by the italics what I have added.

Let's go back to the lion story. Why did the lions eat this fellow? Everyone knows that African lions don't make good pets. Why have them in the first place?

Let me carry the tale a bit further:

In the town that I lived, Monroe, Oregon, we had a man named Paul who kept three lions in his house. This was back in 1979. My father owned a meat company, and every day or two Paul would load his pet lions into the back of his pickup and bring them to our store. There he would buy steaks, beef bones, and bags of dog food to feed to his lions. I actually went out and petted the lions on several occasions, and it always thrilled the out-of-town customers.

Paul was quite wealthy. He built a huge house with a sunken living room, and catwalks along the upper levels gave his lions a nice place to perch while he sat on his bean bags and watched television.

In fact, he bought the lions from a good friend of mine, a fellow named Jack Lawrence, who sold exotic animals as pets and to zoos. Jack used to keep an ostrich in his house in a bird cage, and he always had a couple of Bengal tigers out in his barns, along with a few lions and bears, and even a white buffalo. It turns out that not many people want lions, and so you could buy one back then for about five hundred dollars.

I once asked Paul why he had bought the lions. He told me that he liked the novelty of it. But there were darker rumors in town. Paul had a lot of money, but no job. Folks whispered that he was a drug dealer. He kept the lions, it was said, much in the way that other people keep pit bulls—to keep people away from his house.

I believed the rumors. Paul had an oily look to him, much like a Hollywood movie producer, and he was always anxious, always peering over his shoulder, his eyes darting about.

He had a beautiful wife. Both of them were in their mid-20s, but apparently there were real problems in their marriage. The neighbors complained of screaming fights and bickering.

So the day that Paul got eaten, here is what happened:

He and his wife got in a brawl. No one knows what the fight was about, but the town had its suspicions. There had been reports of gunmen sneaking up on the house two nights before, and Paul had kept his wife locked in for days.

It was said that she wanted him to leave, to take their drugs and money and head to Hawaii.

After the fight, she left the house crying and told Paul that she didn't want to live like that anymore. Then she drove a hundred miles to her parents' house and stayed there for three days.

As she left, Paul yelled at her back, "Yeah, well I'm leaving you! You can keep the damned house!"

As she raced off in her sports car, he leapt into his pickup and sent dirt flying as he sped away.

She refused to call him for the next two days, and he didn't call her.

But she worried about the lions. Had they been fed? African lions are calm when they are well fed, but they get nasty when they're hungry. So she worried.

On Sunday morning, the third day out, she finally called the house. No one picked up. She phoned one of her husband's drug-dealing friends and asked if he had seen Paul. The dealer replied that Paul had stayed at his house until late Saturday night, and then had gone home to feed the lions, but had not returned.

Shaking with trepidation, she drove home and found Paul's pickup outside. She rang the bell, but no one answered. So she carefully entered the house.

She flipped on the lights to the living room and immediately spotted a huge bloodstain on the tan carpet in front of the television. In the center of the bloodstain was all that was left of Paul—the upper half of his skull.

There was speculation that drug dealers had killed Paul, and for a couple of days we wondered.

The police disposed of the lions. They cut the cats open to retrieve enough of Paul's lower skull to check his dental records. It was him. The rest of his body—flesh, hair, hide and bones—were all found inside the lions, too.

There were no signs of foul play—no bullets riddling the body.

Only an idiot would keep lions in his house.

Now, as stories go, this doesn't compare to *Gone with the Wind*. But it does have more of the bare elements of a story. The characters, Paul and his wife (names have been changed to protect the innocent), are brought into the story. They are assigned motives for their actions, motives that might be exaggerated or completely untrue. A problem develops. Both parties become concerned for the lions and return to feed them, hoping to resolve the problem, and one of the two parties is eaten. The story is resolved, of course, only when the lions are destroyed.

This story even has a moral: don't keep lions in your house.

It's obvious why the events within a story need to entertain. After all, you want people to pay you money to make this stuff up!

But it is less obvious why I've added the phrase "The tale answers the question 'Why?'" when I defined a story.

Do stories really need to justify their own existence? Or can we write successful tales that only pose questions?

Time and again, reading through perhaps a hundred textbooks and through my personal study, those who seriously consider plot suggest that in any opening sequence a mystery or puzzle is usually produced, one that the protagonist must resolve.

If the author doesn't resolve that puzzle—if the author leaves the ending open and lets the reader "decide," the tale is nearly always unsatisfying. The reader will not be able to relax himself—return to his original state of rest—until he gets an authoritative answer regarding the resolution. In fact, most readers will feel cheated if the question isn't answered. If you watch a murder mystery, you want to know whodunit. If you're reading a romance, you want to know if the protagonists find true love. If you're reading a historical novel, you want to find out the author's version of what really happened.

In fact, if any questions are left unanswered—as to the motivations of characters, how the protagonists tried to resolve the issues, and so on—the reader will be left agitated, and will thus be angry about the story.

Recent studies show that when we are confronted with a mystery and try to resolve it, the brain releases dopamine in order to reward us for the search. As soon as the answer to the mystery is found, the release of dopamine ceases, and serotonin gets released. In other words, we are rewarded *in part* just for the search, but the biggest reward comes from finding the answer.

So in the opening of every successful story, a mystery or puzzle must be produced, or no story exists at all. Somerset Maugham's little tale about the queen's death doesn't succeed as a story in part because it doesn't create a mystery.

Having said this, I have to consider whether my definition really satisfies you. On the surface, it may sound odd. Why does the story have to answer "Why?"

For example, mysteries are often referred to as "Whodunits," not "Why-dunits." When a dead body is found, the detective immediately sets out to figure out who did it.

But in order to solve the crime, the detective must meet three criteria: he must show the perpetrator's method, his motive, and that he had an opportunity to commit the crime.

Thus, when you find a multimillionaire stabbed in the middle of an airport, you may have ten thousand suspects at first. The detective doesn't need to look far for the method—the guy has a knife sticking out of his back. Nor does he have to consider the question of opportunity. Anyone in the airport has a chance at the victim. Motive becomes the central question in every case.

So a mystery is never finished until the answer to "why?" has been determined. Indeed, if you're reading a mystery and the police have a suspect without a motive, you can be sure that a new suspect will pop up shortly.

In a romance tale, we may believe that most readers are interested in sharing a vicarious love experience. But every romance writer knows that for two characters to be in love, there has to be some attraction. There has to be a reason "why" these two people love one another and get together in the end.

In adventure, it is not enough that the protagonist survive the perils thrown at him. We must answer why. It may be that he's as strong as Conan, has the True Grit of John Wayne, is as clever as McGyver, or has more gadgets than Agent 007.

It really doesn't matter, so long as the hero has some strength, some unusual talent or determination that illustrates why he prevails.

And yet—my basic definition of a story still isn't complete. Nor is the lion story, for that matter. Something is still bothering you, if you've got a keen sense of story.

The first thing that may be bothering you is this: adequate stakes. Who cares about these people anyway? They should never have let lions in the house. Neither of them at this point really has come alive as a character. Do we feel any sympathy toward these fools? And what about the lions? They seem like the real helpless victims here. Maybe the story should be told from the point of view of one of them.

So as writers we can choose to raise the emotional stakes. We could create sympathy for the lions. Maybe our female character has a favorite, a lioness that she raised from a cub. We can create a scene where we show our female protagonist playing with the big cat, and while she grooms her lioness, it purrs and begins to clean the wife's face in turn, licking her with a huge pink tongue.

We can also raise the stakes for our human characters. We show our heroine as a victim. Her husband is a drug dealer, one who has killed rival drug lords to ensure that he keeps his territory. She didn't know what he would become when she married him. It wasn't until after they married that he began to reveal his cruel streak.

He loves his lions, too—not because they're big cuddly kittens, but because they're feral and dangerous, "Just one skipped meal away from reverting to killers," he likes to say.

So our wife regrets her marriage. Her husband is cruel and abusive. Like a lion, he likes to keep a harem of women. Yeah, she's the one he's married to, but there are plenty of others out in the bush.

And the problem is growing. Perhaps the wife sees her husband as some Manson-esque rogue, spending most of his days on LSD, slipping further and further into his own sadistic fantasy world.

Thus, she has been hoping to escape for weeks. She knows that if she stays much longer, he will kill her.

So she finally has a fight, and gets up the courage to leave. Maybe the husband tries to stop her as she lunges for the door. Maybe he slaps her around, but the wife's "kitten" steps between them, warning him back, giving her just enough time to reach the door.

The wife makes her escape, but more than that has to happen. She needs to recognize that her pet is in danger. It isn't enough for her just to escape, she needs her kitten to come with her.

So she has to try to rescue her pet. She might call a neighbor or try to get her husband on the phone and plead with him. She might ask the police to go check on the cats. Whatever she tries, Algis Budrys, a longtime critic for the *Chicago Sun*, would tell you that her first two attempts must be futile.

His model of a story contains the following elements:

—The story must have a character

—In a setting

—With a meaningful conflict (some writers would suggest that the conflict be the most vital conflict that that character will face in his or her lifetime).Others would insist that if you care enough about the protagonist, even small conflicts will feel important.

—The character must then try to resolve the conflict and fail.

—The character must try to resolve the conflict a second time, using greater resources—more resolve, more determination, with a better plan, perhaps even calling upon the aid of friends—and fail a second time.

—The character must make one grand final attempt to resolve the problem. (In some cases, this might well be a life-and-death attempt to resolve the story.) The character may succeed in his or her attempt, or may fail. But we must be convinced that the character did everything possible.

—Somewhere, in the end, there must be a sense of validation that comes from outside the character. Perhaps it is another important character who congratulates your protagonist, or some authority— a doctor or a policeman—who looks at the fallen body of the enemy and pronounces the villain dead.

Here is a chart that shows the modified Feralt's Triangle as it now stands.

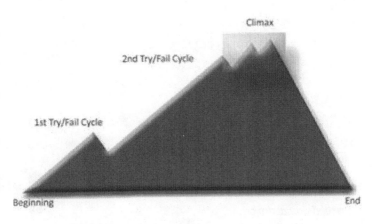

Now, Algis Budrys didn't invent his definition of a story. It was commonly used by writers in the 1950s. In fact, one large company of agents used to send a similar plot chart and definition to writers in an attempt to teach them how to plot stories.

You will note that I have a blue box at the top of my chart. That blue box represents a reversal. This is an apparent ending—one where the hero suddenly finds himself defeated, but quickly turns the table on the villain and wins the day. Popular movies that feature such reversals include *Avatar*, *Live Free or Die Hard*, and *Jurassic Park*.

The important difference between Feralt's Triangle and the above chart, of course, is that there must be attempts made to resolve a problem, and they must fail. If you read a story where the protagonist succeeds on the first attempt, invariably you will sense that the problem wasn't really that big after all. In other words, it didn't have the heft needed to carry the story. The same is true if only two attempts are needed to succeed. For some reason innate to human chemistry, the hero must attempt to resolve the problem at least three times. Having them try six or seven will most likely be overkill, but even those can work. Remember the movie *Groundhog Day*?

There are other examples of what one might call "near stories" that don't work, usually because there aren't enough try/fail cycles. Let me give you one, a story told by a friend long ago:

I was in the airport a few weeks ago in Portland, Oregon, and I met a world-famous pianist, Edvard Van Eyck. He was in a terribly foul mood.

It seems that he was supposed to be giving a concert that night, a huge benefit to help AIDS victims in Africa. But a few days earlier, his mother had a bad stroke.

Now, Van Eyck always performs on one of his own pianos, and he had his blue Steinway shipped from Denmark two days before the performance. He got it to the performance centre, but it was raining terribly in Oregon, with 100 percent humidity, and by the time that it reached the hall, his assistant determined that the piano was out of tune.

Van Eyck always insists on tuning his own pianos, but he dared not leave his mother alone for long. Even though she was recovering, he wanted to stay by her side.

But by sheer chance, his assistant made a few phone calls and discovered that they were in luck. Perhaps the world's most renowned piano-maker happened to be in town, hoping to hear the performance. The man, a famous Greek fellow named Gregor Oppornockity, said, "Don't worry about a thing. I will have the piano tuned to perfection."

Of course, in the humidity, the cat-gut strings had stretched and loosened, and Gregor spent several hours tuning the piano, tightening and replacing the strings as needed. He finished late at night.

But only hours before the performance, a huge storm hit, and lightning struck the skylight at the event centre, shattering the glass. Rain fell on the piano, and in a matter of moments all of Gregor's work was undone.

Fortunately, as Van Eyck was flying out of Brooklyn, his assistant was able to call the tuner and beg him to rush back to work on the broken instrument. If he worked quickly, Van Eyck knew, the heaters could be placed on the stage to dry the piano, and the strings could be re-tuned before they needed to be replaced.

It was not until the great Van Eyck landed in Portland that he got the bad news. The headstrong Dane had refused to save the day, and as a result the event was doomed. Van Eyck's assistant told how he had pleaded with Gregor to come save the day, but resisting all pleas and offers, Gregor shouted, "You should know, Oppornockity only tunes once!"

Now, you will notice that the previous narrative has many earmarks of a story. It has a protagonist, a setting, and problem. There is an attempt to resolve the problem—possibly even two attempts.

Then the writer hits you with the joke ending.

This form of story is called a *jape*, and part of the reason that it lures you in is because you imagine that you are listening to a story. You expect the narrative to reach a certain kind of conclusion. Instead, it's a joke ending, often with a pun.

Let me suggest a couple of other ways to look at stories that could be helpful in the following section.

ON STORY TYPES VERSUS SHAPES

Very often writers try to categorize stories into "types" in order to understand how they work. Thus, we might talk about "boy-meets-girl" romances or "revenge" plots. But some critics have pointed out that stories can also be defined by "shape."

Most authors don't visualize their stories as shapes, but I've learned to see stories as shapes over the years, and often I envision them in rather complex forms.

Here are a few common shapes.

The Serial or Episodic Plot—a zigzag line, a series of Feralt Triangles set end to end.

This is used for stories that aren't meant to come to an end. Instead, the characters go from one adventure to the next, often without any real growth. This plot worked fine for novels at one time, and was used extensively in pulp fiction, in weekly serial novels for newspapers, in early radio shows. It is now used mainly in television. An episode of *Two And a Half Men* is represented by a single triangle, while the series can be seen as the overall diagram—extending out over hundreds of episodes. Here, known characters are put in a known setting and given new problems to solve each week, usually without referencing past problems (though a series may have an overarching conflict that is sometimes addressed through two or three episodes).

The Journey Home, or Cyclic Plot—an arrow drawn in a circle shape, ending where it began.

This plot takes us through a tale and returns the hero or heroine to his or her doorstep, with all of the adventures eventually meaning ... not quite nothing. Perhaps the apprentice becomes a wizard, and in turn takes a new apprentice and initiates the cycle all over again, or the young girl has adventures, marries, and in time raises her own daughter. The cyclic journey is the point of the story. Examples include Ursula K. LeGuin's *Always Coming Home* and Hemingway's *The Sun Also Rises*.

The Onion-Skin or Chinese Puzzle plot—an onion, with a kernel at the center and layers and layers encompassing it.

This plot usually is a mystery tale. As each outer layer is peeled away, as each mystery is resolved, it leads to a deeper mystery, with one central truth at its heart. If the writer is a cynic or a mystic, the central truth may be that "the quest for truth is unending, and all questions eventually lead to a greater mystery." Sometimes, the mysteries are completely unrelated to one another.

As you consider plot shapes, you'll notice that with any one of them, the seven-point plot plan may be used internally. In short, all that the shape does is to tell us where the character ends in relation to where he or she began.

So not all tales are completely linear. They may zigzag or circle around on you.

One Last Way to Look at Plot

For some authors, it is hard to think of plots in terms of try/fail cycles. It may seem too contrived, too linear and artificial. Indeed, not everything that happens in life belongs to a story, even when the story is true.

For example, in our lion tale, I might find myself writing a scene in which our heroine, having left her husband, finds herself fleeing through the night in the mountains. While driving over the gravel road, I might imagine her blowing a front tire.

Afraid that her husband is following her, she pulls off into the brush on a dirt road and sets about trying to fix her tire.

What does it have to do with the try/fail cycles of the story? Perhaps nothing. The entire scene could easily be deleted from the tale without affecting it adversely. In short, some might consider it to be a structural flaw.

But maybe it gives my heroine time to worry, to think, to grow afraid. Maybe she remembers hearing about mountain lions in the neighborhood, and I can draw the tale back toward a recurring theme.

This incident thrown into the tale might help in no other way than to create verisimilitude—a sense that the story is really happening, that this isn't a contrived piece of fiction. Or it may be that the incident serves as an emotional beat, creating a new note that resonates in the author's "emotional symphony" that makes up a longer tale.

Many great tales have such contrived incidents in them. Look at *Lord of the Rings*. What does Tom Bombadil's episode have to do with the overall story? Many critics have said that it could be deleted easily, and that the overall novel would be better. But by taking Bombadil out, the story would immediately become far more linear, and therefore feel more contrived.

This leads toward another valuable way to look at a story: as a series of incidents that happen to a character, requiring the character's response.

At the beginning of a story, a character may simply be lying in bed. Let's make him a boy, age 12. But something throws him out of bed. Maybe it's a tornado that comes whirling over the prairie, hurling his trailer house into the air and sucking his family away, so that he is left alone in the universe.

Maybe the thing that hits him is his drunken father who insists that it's time for the boy to grow up and "start makin' yer own way!"

In either case, this opening scenario is what is called the "inciting incident" to the story. A child has lost his home, and must try to find happiness out in a cruel and uncaring world.

Perhaps as an author, you don't think about how he might try finding happiness in life too much. The first thing that he might go looking for is food or shelter. Maybe he needs to ascertain whether his family is alive.

Depending upon what type of character you create, his actions may differ wildly. So he responds to the incident.

Of course as he responds, other things are bound to happen. Maybe he just decides to curl up under a wind-fallen tree for the night. What happens when he does? In the morning he wakes, cold and hungry.

So he goes looking for food, responding to his hunger, and sneaks into a town where he tries to steal a loaf of bread. All of the sudden, a woman catches him and shouts, "Thief!"

Suddenly we have a new incident, a new stimulus for our character, and he will have to respond to that stimulus.

Using the incident/reaction model for writing is often an easy way to generate a story, and some classics—like *Gulliver's Travels*—probably came about this way.

At the same time, ultimately such a story will tend to get bogged down as trivial incidents arise in the writer's mind and find their way onto paper.

Still, if you as a writer find yourself stuck for a bit—if you're writing a story and can't quite make out what should happen in the long run, it doesn't hurt to revert to this method for a scene or two as you let your subconscious work out the answer to your problems.

DEFINING A MILLION-DOLLAR PROPERTY

A Million Dollar Property is one that can and should make you a million dollars.

Years ago, I was driving through Scotland when I came up with the idea for the magic systems in my *Runelords* novels. The magic system was complex and unique, and it struck me all at once.

Immediately, I had the thought, "This could be worth a million dollars!" But after a moment's thought, I realized, "No, this is worth a lot more than that!"

That was 15 years ago. The property has indeed brought in more than a million dollars. It has brought in more than two. I'm working hard to make my third million from it. I expect to make much more.

That's the way most of us authors make our million. We sell a book in the U.S., begin selling foreign rights, make a movie deal or two, and our fortunes grow by accretion. Most successful authors build their career around one or two major intellectual properties.

But it doesn't have to work that way. Sometimes you can write a story that will make you a million dollars right out the gate. Indeed, if you look at Stephenie Meyer or J.K. Rowling, you'll see authors who have created first properties that made hundreds of millions of dollars.

My friend Kevin J. Anderson used some of the techniques that we're discussing here, and he was able to write a novel called *Ignition* that got picked up by a major publisher and movie company for a million dollars in cold, hard cash. Now, the movie never got made, and when the book came out it didn't get much promotion. So the author had to console himself with his fortune.

That's the caveat here. You can do your part, but when your book comes out, there are a lot of things that will be beyond your control—things like how the cover looks, what it is sold for, how much promotion the publisher puts into it, where it appears on the publisher's sales list, who you're facing as competition that month, and so on. In fact, of all the factors that make a successful book, you may only be able to control one—the quality of your story.

So you can, quite literally, create a property that is worth millions of dollars and have your publishers and movie studios blow it.

If that happens, then you can use this guide to help you create another million-dollar intellectual property.

That's the beauty of it. We're writers. We're creators. If we need to, we can dust ourselves off and start over again.

WHY DO RESEARCH FOR BECOMING A BESTSELLER?

Many times when a writer starts to write his or her first book, it is because the seed of an idea takes root in his or her head and the author feels that it must come out. This is the author's primary motivation to write.

That's not a bad way to write, but unfortunately in many cases the new author will pen something that feels terribly important and profound to him or her while the rest of the world might not respond at all. That's because so many new authors write as a type of therapy. We write about conflicts and situations that resonate with us personally instead of the world at large. (See my book, *Drawing on the Power of Resonance in Writing*.)

The new author, after two or three sales, will often find him or herself sliding back down on the sales charts, and only then will begin to wonder what it is that the rest of the world would like to see in a story. Hence, many authors fail in their careers after only a couple of books.

The answer to that question—What does the reader want?—of course changes from reader to reader. But if you're looking to sell big, you need to begin doing some research.

My research process requires me to look not just at book sales, but also at popular movies and television shows, even videogames and comics—to try to get a snapshot of our culture as a whole.

The reason for this is quite simple. If I write a book, there are a limited number of readers for it. For example, it has been estimated that in my own field, fantasy, there are only about two or three million regular readers out there. I can catch some of those people as they wander past my books, but if I want to go really big—say *Harry Potter* big—I need to do better than that. I need to create a sensation. I need to get enough publicity on morning television and radio shows so that it drives readers into the bookstore—the way that Rowling, Paolini, and Meyer recently have done.

In order to appeal to that wider audience, I look at several mediums and try to take some clues from them.

Audience Analysis: Film

For many years, in the United States a hit movie has been defined as one that grosses $100 million in the domestic box office. In order for a movie to gross $100 million at the box office, it has to draw a viewership of about 16 million people—which is much larger than the number of hardcover sales made by almost any novel.

So, what can you learn by studying viewer's movie tastes? A few years ago I read a book on screenwriting. In it, the instructor listed the top 50 bestselling movies of all time and asked that you look for similarities. When I reached the end of the list, the author announced that there were *no* similarities. But I had found three things that they all had in common. The list has changed in the past ten years, but my points will still hold true. In fact, I've even found a few more similarities.

Here is the list of top box office movies in the US (as of 2012):

Top Grossing Movies Worldwide (in thousands)

1—*Avatar* (2009)
$2,782.3
2—*Titanic* (1997)
$2,185.4
3—*The Avengers* (2012)
$1,511.8
4—Harry Potter and the Deathly Hallows Part 2 (2011)
$1,328.1
5—Transformers: Dark of the Moon (2011)
$1,123.7
6—The Lord of the Rings: Return of the King (2003)
$1,119.9
7—The Dark Knight Rises (2012)
$1,081.0
8—Pirates of the Caribbean: Dead Man's Chest (2006)
$1,066.2
9—*Toy Story 3* (2010)
$1,063.2
10—Pirates of the Caribbean: On Stranger Tides (2011)
$1,043.9
11—Star Wars: The Phantom Menace (1999)
$1,027.0

12—*Alice in Wonderland* (2010)
$1,024.3

13—*Skyfall* (2012)
$1,023.7

14—*The Dark Knight* (2008)
$1,004.6

15—Harry Potter and the Sorcerer's Stone (2001)
$974.8

16—Pirates of the Caribbean: At World's End (2007)
$963.4

17—Harry Potter and the Deathly Hallows Part 1
(2010)
$956.4

18—*The Lion King* (1994)
$951.6

19—Harry Potter and the Order of the Phoenix (2007)
$939.9

20—Harry Potter and the Half-Blood Prince (2009)
$934.4

21—Lord of the Ring: The Two Towers (2002)
$926.0

22—*Finding Nemo* (2003)
$921.7

23—*Shrek 2* (2004)
$919.8

24—*Jurassic Park* (1993)
$914.7

25—Harry Potter and the Goblet of Fire (2005)
$896.9

26—*Spider-Man 3* (2007)
$890.9

27—Ice Age: Dawn of the Dinosaurs (2009)
$886.7

28—Harry Potter and the Chamber of Secrets (2002)
$879.0

29—Ice Age: Continental Drift (2012)
$875.2

30—The Lord of the Rings: Fellowship of the Ring (2001)
$871.5

31—Star Wars: Episode III Revenge of the Sith (2005)
$848.8

32—Transformers: Revenge of the Fallen (2009)
$836.3

33—The Hobbit: An Unexpected Journey (2012)
$829.5

34—*Inception* (2010)
$825.5

35—The Twilight Saga: Breaking Dawn Part 2 (2012)
$821.8

36—*Spider-Man* (2002)
$821.7

37—*Independence Day* (1996)
$817.4

38—*Shrek the Third* (2007)
$799.0

39—Harry Potter and the Prisoner of Azkaban (2004)
$796.7

40—E.T.: The Extra Terrestrial (1982)
$792.9

41—Indiana Jones: Kingdom of the Crystal Skull (2008)
$786.6

42—*Spider-Man 2* (2004)
$783.8

43—*Star Wars* (1977)
$775.4

44—*2012* (2009)
$769.7

45—*The Da Vinci Code* (2006)
$758.2

46—Shrek Forever After (2010)
$752.6

47—The Amazing Spider-Man (2012)
$752.2

48—The Chronicles of Narnia: The Lion, the Witch,
and the Wardrobe (2005)
$745.0

49—The Matrix Reloaded (2003)
$742.1

50—Madagascar 3: Europe's Most Wanted (2012)
$742.1

The list above has not been corrected for inflation, so the sales are skewed a little more toward recent movies than they should be, but they're accurate enough. Also, the rankings will shift as new big movies come out. So what do these films have in common?

Here are a few things:

—Movies Set in Another Time and/or Another Place: 94%.

This tells us that movies that take us away from the real world and *transport* us into an alternate reality are far more popular than those set within a contemporary setting.

—Movies with Wide Audience Potential (Male/female): 98%.

Most of these movies have strong protagonists of both sexes and of various ages. Thus they draw in a much wider audience than, say, a teen chick flick that only attracts young women. However, the main story focus is almost always on a relatively young male—anywhere from a child to a man in his early twenties. I hate that statistic (because it suggests that only young men can draw huge audiences, and logically I know that that is a fallacy), but I can't ignore it.

—Movies with High Emotional Richter-Scale Values: 100%.

A movie that scores high on the "emotional Richter scale" is often among the best of its kind. If it's supposed to be scary, it's terrifying. If it's supposed to funny, you laugh so hard that you can't breathe. If it's an adventure, it's heart-pounding. This is important. If you want to really please an audience, you need to know how your work stacks up in the marketplace.

The movies here tend to tug on the heartstrings. Very often they achieve this by placing an entire "world" in jeopardy. But sometimes, as in *Home Alone* or *Forrest Gump*, the movie focuses on one very likable protagonist—then puts him or her through hell.

Movies with Heroic Main Plot: 98%.

Almost every movie on the list focuses on someone who is trying to save others.

Fantasy or Science Fiction: 90%.

Since I write fantasy I'd like to point out that fantasy movies have been topping the bestseller lists for decades. It's time that the studios take notice!

Alternate World: 80%.

Most of these movies that have done well have been set in an alternate world, not in our world.

So, as a writer, what can you learn from these points? Well, if you're trying to write a bestseller, this information might be something of a treasure map, pointing you in some likely directions.

How Accurate is the Above Research?

In the research above, I made some comments that caused at least one reader to say, "Whoa, are you sure about that?" In particular I pointed out that in the top 50 movies, although we often see the story told from multiple points of view, all of these movies tend to put most of their focus on the male characters' journey.

Does that mean that you have to focus on men? Really? More than half the people on this planet are women—about 51 percent of them.

So my reader pointed out that the data may be biased, and I agreed that she is absolutely right. In fact, while writing the article, I almost wanted to stop and give you a caveat but I decided against it. You see as someone who was trained as a scientist I think that there is value in saying, "This is what I observe," regardless of whether I believe the observation will lead to valid conclusions.

At the same time, I want you to understand that I strongly believe that the data does tend to be biased. Here are a couple of reasons why: first, if you look at the list of the top 50 movies of all time, you'll note that they are predominantly special-effects heavy movies. The budgets on such movies are huge—$100 to 200 million.

Let's take the one of bestselling movies of all time from this list: *Titanic*. The movie went way over budget and cost more than $200 million to make. The special-effects budget was huge. My good friend Grant Boucher created the digital ship used in the sinking scene and won an Oscar for it, so I know some of the effort that he put into that effect. Cameron had tried a couple of different ways to get the picture he wanted—creating a large model ship and then using a real ship. Neither delivered the image that he had hoped for, so Grant spent six months secretly building a 3-D model of the ship, and then slipped some footage with it into the mix. Add in a $6 million program to create digital water and—voila!—you're winning Oscars.

But in order to earn back the huge amounts of money spent on such a movie, the studio had to advertise heavily. In fact, the movie was released simultaneously in Europe, Asia, and England all on the same weekend in order to begin retrieving the profits.

On a normal movie that goes out for theatrical distribution the advertising often runs about $8 million. But that money can easily go up to $20 million, and of course if you've got $200 million into the film, you can easily spend $100 million on advertising.

So movies with huge budgets get heavy advertising—which then makes them into hits.

When you see a Star Wars Episode VI on the list of top-selling films of all time, or a Pirates of the Caribbean 3, what it really means is that the studios went on an all-out blitz on advertising in order to garner viewers.

Movies were filmed, but maybe books were written in conjunction with the film—as many as 27 different books to help hype *Star Wars* Episode 1. These books then act as free advertisements for the film. Video games also get made, advertised, and unleashed on the public. Thus when the last *Matrix* film was made, a record $55 million was spent on the game tie in. On top of those forms of advertising, entire magazines maybe started in order to hype the coming films (an old friend of mine founded the company that initiated this form of advertising years ago by creating the first Star Wars magazine). T-shirts and toy lines are created so that you will see movie ads in clothing and toy stores— not to mention the other merchandise, such as key chains, hats, wallpaper, underwear, and so on. Then there are the cross-promotions—the free Star Wars toys at McDonalds, the Shrek ads displayed on Pepsi cans, the new cereal lines, and so on.

Given the hundreds of millions of dollars in advertisement, it's no wonder that the movie does well.

Of course, all of these ads and cross promotions are easily justifiable. If a movie has enough multimedia appeal it can pull in billions of dollars. The Star Wars movies, for example, might make the filmmakers a few hundred million, but the Star Wars merchandise tie-ins make Lucas $3 to 5 billion per film.

But what about films that don't have game tie-ins? If they had huge advertising budgets, would they make a lot of money? I suspect so. For example, lots of kids watched High School Musical over and over again. If Disney were to take High School Musical 4, release it in theaters, and give it the same promotional budget that they gave to Pirates of the Caribbean 3, the box office sales would likely go through the roof.

So the "bestseller" list is skewed toward big-budget films.

Other factors also lead to skewed information. For example, in most cases these movies are made by men for men. The producers, the studio execs, the directors—all of them are men. There might be a female director somewhere in the top 50 but I don't recall any. So men tend to create the kinds of movies that will appeal to other men. That's why, I believe, that even though the main plot line in each of the top 50 movies is slanted toward a hero-journey story, I strongly suspect that it doesn't have to be.

As evidence of that, look on the bestseller list for books recently. At the time that I'm writing this, *USA Today* has

Stephanie Meyer at four of the ten top spots, and her books are definitely not slanted toward the male audience.

The same skew toward the male audience can be seen in the videogame industry. If you go to E3, you'll see thousands of games that are being developed by various companies—almost all of which are targeted toward the young male audience. Why? Because the guys who run the videogame companies are young men! But if you look at the games that really succeed hugely you'll note that the games are aimed at a much wider audience—male and female—and are skewed particularly to younger players.

So one has to wonder just how valid the observations I made about the films are. The answer is that they're perfectly valid *If you want to make a blockbuster movie*. The studios are still run by men. The producers are mostly men. Most of the biggest directors are men, and the truth is that these guys in Hollywood tend to be very superstitious about films. If something has worked before, they think it will work again. So if they're going to back a film, it had better fit into the parameters of set by other blockbusters.

But the observations aren't all necessarily valid for other mediums—such as books and television.

Given this, let's go to another medium and see if we can learn something from it. Here is a list of the current top 10 shows (at the time of my writing this).

- *Big Bang Theory*
- *Person of Interest*
- *Two and a Half Men*
- *NCIS*
- *Revolution*
- *Voice*
- *Chicago Fire*
- *The Following*

- *Carrie Diaries*
- *Vegas*

In this list, we see something interesting. The amazing thing to me is how this list of last week's top shows differs in content from our movies. In short, we don't have any alternate world science fiction television shows among the top 20, whereas the movie results would predict that we should have them.

Television tends to be cheap. The special effects needed to create an alternate world show are too costly to use. So the closest that we get in our list is a near-future science fiction piece. In the past few years, television shows like *Heroes*, *Buffy*, and *The Sarah Conner Chronicles* have been high in the top ten, but they also used minimal effects. But on this week reality crime dramas seemed to be the big ticket. It makes me wonder if I should be writing murder mysteries.

But the answer is no. I just gave you the results for last week, not for the entire year. The results for each week are skewed because we have more than one television "season" per year.

In short, if you study television, you'll notice that shows that get a lot of hype during the week tend to come out near the top of the polls at the week's end. Crime dramas, comedy, and reality television all top our charts.

As in the movies, advertising proves its worth.

Now, you can get lots of television ratings information over the web. You can get it sorted by viewers in various regions, by color, and so on. You can get lists of the best soap operas, the top crime dramas, or favorite game shows. You can even get lists that show the most popular science fiction and fantasy tales. Luckily, you can even get actual numbers that show how many viewers watch a particular show.

But beware: television seasons are short nowadays, running only for a few months. So *American Idol* will be at the top one week and off the charts the next simply because there is no new episode coming out.

So what good does it do you to understand that the vice presidential debate pulled in 30 million viewers? Well, it's great news if you're releasing a book on Mitt Romney that week. It means that you'll have 30 million people who might be curious to learn a little more about him. As a writer it can give you a hint at how large your potential audience might be and it can determine the date for when your book should be released. If you knew six weeks in advance when the debate was coming, you'd make sure to do some huge promotions at that time—speaking on Rush Limbaugh and whatnot.

More than that, knowing that a television show is huge can let you see if you have a ready-made audience. So in 2011 *Game of Thrones* had the number one spot in fictive television if I recall, with 40 million viewers watching the opening episode.

So imagine that you wrote a book that would appeal to that audience. We know that only about 50 percent of the people in this country will read any book this year. Given that information you can estimate that your book has a potential audience of 20 million people. That's a huge audience. With enough advertising, you could make millions on that book. But of course you won't be able to reach all of your prospective buyers. After all, you don't own your own television network. You can't advertise to them in a manner that is cost-effective. But an audience that size does give you something to build on.

Let's go back to one of our bestselling authors in the U.S., Stephanie Meyer. She built her audience this way, whether she knows it or not.

You see, the final episode of *Buffy the Vampire Slayer* aired on May 20 of 2003. Buffy usually held a viewership of 4 to 6 million people per week, sometimes spiking much higher than that, and it ran for six years. What does that have to do with Stephanie Meyer?

Well, its departure created a void for fans of the show. But less than two weeks later, on June 2 of 2003, Stephanie Meyers records that she had a vivid dream that led her to begin writing *Twilight*. In her dream, a young woman was having an engrossing conversation with a vampire that loved her.

Stephanie's timing was excellent. Other marketing factors were also in play. A popular movie series based upon Anne Rice's tales had just finished with *Queen of the Damned* (2002), and so vampires were hot. Meanwhile, the movie *Underworld*—with the vampire versus werewolf conflict used by Meyer—was just beginning to advertise in the theaters for its September release. So when Stephenie sent her book in, it was precisely the kind of thing that plenty of readers were looking for.

In fact, when Stephenie took my writing class at BYU in 2001, we talked a bit about how she should approach the markets, and we discussed how the timing for this kind of novel would work well.

From time to time, we see a television series that has wide appeal and which gets canceled anyway (think *Touched by an Angel*, *Heroes*, or *Buffy*). When that happens, it leaves audiences wanting.

If you're an enterprising writer, you can step in and fill the void in the lives of the shows' fans.

AUDIENCE ANALYSIS: NOVELS

In considering how to approach this topic, it seemed to me that there are some things that I could teach you, or there are things that you can teach yourself. In other words, I sometimes believe that you learn better by doing. So instead of analyzing some bestsellers, I'm going to give you a list of books and show you how I would approach those books to see what kinds of things they have in common. But you should do your own analysis. In other words, I'd like you to learn how to think.

So here is a list of the 20 bestselling novels of all time. This is a list that covers books read by both young adults and adults. So there aren't any picture books in it for example. The books and the numbers are taken from Wikipedia, and the list is obviously wrong in at least one instance. The list shows *Harry Potter and the Deathly Hallows* high on the list but doesn't show the first book in the series, *Harry Potter and the Sorcerer's Stone* anywhere at all. Since the first books in a series will always outpace the last books in sales (because there is always some falloff), it is obvious that we've got a problem. Furthermore, sales of the *Harry Potter* books hit over 400 million for the series as a whole several years ago. With seven books in the series, that means we have average sales of near 60 million copies, not the 44 million listed as top sales here. In short, all seven books in the series should be on this list, not just the last book, and the numbers should range higher.

In any case, the list should still be instructive:

1—*A Tale of Two Cities* by Charles Dickens
2—*The Lord of the Rings* by J. R. R. Tolkien
3—And Then There Were None by Agatha Christie
4—*The Hobbit* by J. R. R. Tolkien
5—*She* by H. Rider Haggard
6—The Catcher in the Rye by J. D. Salinger
7—*The Alchemist* by Paulo Coelho
8—The Da Vinci Code by Dan Brown
9—The Name of the Rose by Umberto Eco
10—Harry Potter and the Deathly Hallows by J.K. Rowling
11—Jonathon Livingston Seagull by Richard Bach
12—To Kill a Mockingbird by Harper Lee
13—*Valley of the Dolls* by Jacqueline Susann
14—*Gone with the Winde* by Margaret Mitchell
15—*One Hundred Years of Solitude* by Gabriel Garcia Marquez
16—*The Godfather* by Mario Puzo
17—*Jaws* by Peter Benchley
18—*Shogun* by James Clavell
19—The Pillars of the Earth by Ken Follett
20—*Perfume* by Patrick Suskind

Now, given the list above, look for the similarities, for patterns, in order to determine the elements that make a bestseller.

Settings

Let's start with the settings. How many of the books distance the reader from current time and space?

You'll notice that the first book on our list take place six decades before the readers of the 1860s were around. Most of the readers wouldn't have been alive. It would be like me writing about World War II. Also, the book is set in two countries—England and France. In other words, no matter where you were living, the book offered some escape from the contemporary setting.

As you scroll through the list, you'll notice that about 35 percent of the novels are set in complete fantasy worlds. Most of the rest had historical ties. In each case where the novel doesn't distance the reader from the modern world, nearly all of the novels take you someplace that you would like to go—a seaside resort, an island retreat, and so on.

So offering your reader escape seems to be something that most bestsellers have in common. In fact, if you read *Writing the Blockbuster Novel*, Al Zuckerman will tell you that you should look to set your tale in places where the reader might want to go—exotic destinations like Paris, New York, and Saint Petersburg.

But what if you don't want to set your book in one of those places? That's all right, too. You can still entice your reader into your setting. For example, if I were setting a novel in Rigby, Idaho I might consider talking about the things that make Rigby one of the great destinations in the world—clear sunny skies, neighbors with high values, wild elk bedding down on the banks of the Snake River, and so on. In other words, make sure that the setting is a place you want to visit.

This is a key even in my genre of fantasy. Tolkien sold a lot of books, but one of the real reasons why is that Middle-earth is a great place to visit. The Shire with its gentle

Hobbits, its bounteous gardens, and its innocence is an alluring place to go if you want to get away from real-world stress, and as the real-world civil unrest of the 1960s became unbearable, many readers found refuge in Middle-earth.

Beyond just the initial setting though, there are other questions to study. For example, does the setting move about? Or does the novel span dozens or even thousands of years? It's an easy thing for an author to talk about how glacial ice sculpted a present-day valley, or to throw in a story told by a grandmother to help set a scene. All of these techniques can expand the world that you're creating.

Characters

Well, given this list, take a look at the characters in bestsellers. What is the age and sex of each protagonist? Ninety percent of these novels seem to be aimed primarily at men. Some of this may be a throwback to the time when most books were bought by men.

Does the book have more than one major protagonist (usually defined by viewpoint character)?

Does the age of the protagonist change throughout the book? For example, in *Harry Potter* we first meet young Harry shortly after birth, but most of the book takes place later in life.

Beyond age and sex, you might study the characters closely. What is their social status? What about their physical appearances? What kinds of personality traits do they have in common?

Conflicts

After you study the characters, move on to conflicts. I like to take each major character in turn and study each of his or her conflicts. I label them as primary, secondary, tertiary, and so on.

So the next question is a bit tougher. How important to the reader will that conflict be? For example, when *A Tale of Two Cities* was written, the entire world was still reeling from the after-effects of the French Revolution. British nobility—indeed leaders around the entire world—were afraid of losing their heads, and so they began to vie to for the title of "most virtuous leader alive today." Nobles began giving money to charity and making sure that the press was present to see them do it, and so on. The reform movement swept across the oceans to America, where in the 1830s through the 1850s tens of thousands of Christian communes rose up. (I'll bet that you thought communes were a modern thing, something that happened just during the reform of the 1970s, but they go back thousands of years, and I wouldn't be surprised to see them rise up again in the coming decade in response to the global recession.) So the global reform movement swept throughout Europe and Russia, and thus we can see that for a reader in the mid-1800s, this kind of novel struck the reader deeply. In short, it carried information vital to the reader's survival.

We can see that trend toward valuable information throughout the list. Is *Lord of the Rings* really just escapism? I don't think so. As a teenager I clearly believed that the ring of power was a metaphor for the nuclear bomb. Tolkien denies it, but the bulk of the novel was written in the post-war era after WWII. If nothing else, I found myself identifying strongly with the inconsequential hobbits who were trying to rid the world of an item that could destroy them.

How important is it to you to know how the mob works today? When *The Godfather* was released, most people were totally ignorant at how powerful organized crime was. Today we're better educated, but I think that most people would be shocked at just how corrupt politics has become.

So study the conflicts. One screenwriting doctor claims that in every great story, there is a question about the character's identity at its heart. Who am I? Who do others think that I am? This might seem like a tertiary conflict in many of these stories, but I think that you'll find that it is a common thread. In short, pay attention to even the smallest conflicts in the tale.

Very often, a powerful novel doesn't just challenge the protagonist's identity, it challenges the reader's identity, too.

Emotional Beats

In order to sell to any audience, you need to understand what drives that audience. A child may be looking for stories of wonder, tales that have comforting endings. A teen will be more likely to be looking for romance. An older male might be interested in figuring out how to best take care of his family, and so tales that have a strong tie to obtaining wealth become attractive, while older women in particular are interested in stories about belonging.

I worked with a greenlighting company in Hollywood for a few years that used to study how the emotional beats generated in an advertisement campaign would translate into filled seats at the box office. Depending upon the age and sex of the viewer, we could tell what they wanted to see.

So we broke those emotional beats down into certain categories: mystery, drama, romance, adventure, wonder, horror, humor, and lust.

Using this system, we could look at a commercial and say: okay, your primary audience is teen girls. We know that 92 percent of that audience will be driven to the theater to view a movie that has romance in it, while 89 percent are looking for comedy. If the movie hits those emotions, then it will have a large potential audience. On the other hand, what if it hits the wrong emotional markers for the audience? Teenage girls don't generally look for drama; they get enough of it in their lives. Nor do they respond well to pornography. So what if you give them a movie that deals with things that the audience doesn't like? Well, you will probably drive viewers away. Instead of appealing to 90 percent of your audience, if you make a pornographic movie for girls you'll be advertising to less than five percent of them. So your sales will drop dramatically.

Themes

Emotional markers are big in Hollywood, but the list of markers isn't as helpful as it could be. There are commonalities in stories that go beyond the emotional tags, and I'm going to label them as "themes."

I've noticed that tales about character growth tend to be more satisfying than those that are not. So I add that into my mix of things to look for.

Similarly, many readers respond well to novels about friendship—gaining and keeping friends. If you look at the "top television shows of all time" you'll see that many of them—shows like *Cheers*, *M.A.S.H.*, *Seinfeld*, *I Love Lucy*, *Happy Days*, and so on all revolved around a small cluster of friends and cohorts.

As I mentioned above, as a man I've noticed that tales about "making it rich" are attractive to me. Interestingly, before I got married I was far more interested in romance—how to find and wed the right girl. Now my fantasies tend to revolve around, "How am I going to support my family—not just for the rest of my life, but even after I die?"

So look at the bestselling novels of all time. How many of them deal with themes appropriate to their audience?

Miscellaneous

Look at the books above and ask yourself what length has to do with becoming a bestseller. I suspect that when *Lord of the Rings* came out, it was perhaps the longest fantasy novel ever published. But most of the books on the list above are big, honking novels of a quarter of a million words or more. Most of them are among the longest books of their kind.

Why is that? Orson Scott Card has pointed out that when you write a novel of transport—one that takes the reader into another time, place, or culture—it naturally takes longer to tell the story.

But I think that there is more to it. I think that a longer novel invites greater depth. It allows the author to put more characters into deeper conflict, bringing in wider themes, weaving a tapestry that becomes more engrossing to the readers than a shorter work can produce.

Beyond novel length, look at things like: length of chapters and length of scenes.

You could easily go into the mechanics of a bestseller. How much dialog does the author use compared to, say, narration?

Is the book written in first person, second, third? How deeply does the author penetrate into the character's viewpoint? How well is voice used?

You might even get down to smaller elements. In bestselling novels, there is a tendency for authors to dwell upon things such as: what it's like to eat at a restaurant that only the very wealthy can afford. You might study things such as: how does the author handle a dining scene?

Summary

I'd like you to become a student of what sells, and I think that the only way to do it is to do as I have suggested here: create a list of the bestsellers in your genre and medium, then begin to study the commonalities.

As you do this, you'll gain a tremendous advantage over not just the new authors that you meet but even some authors who are widely published. I know dozens of authors who've never given an hour's thought to audience analysis—even authors who have written 30 novels or more.

Some authors have an inner sense of style that allows them to naturally drift toward writing for a wide audience. But most of us have to work a little harder to get a grip on such things.

USING EMOTIONAL DRAWS

In Hollywood, while studying greenlighting for films, I learned that we can predict how well a screenplay will perform based upon its emotional appeal.

The movie studios found that by creating short trailers and testing how well they drew in an audience in the first two weeks of release, we could eventually predict how well a film will do.

Of course, every viewer is an individual, and their tastes will vary.

Overall, we can predict how well an audience will respond to a film based upon several criteria—the view's age, the viewer's sex, and the type of emotional appeals that the trailer creates.

To give you an idea of what I mean, let's analyze an audience by age.

When you're a child—between the ages of 0 and 11—you're in what I will call the "discovery" phase of life, a time when much of the world seems strange and new to you. In some ways, the world seems boundless, because every time that you turn around you learn about some new wonder or some new region of the world that you have never heard about. So children in that age are predisposed to what I, and a few others, call "wonder literature."

In wonder literature, the main emotional draw (outside of the essential story itself) is typically that it arouses a sense of wonder. Hence, stories set in fantastic settings are extremely interesting to children. But when you encounter something new—say a new animal—there is more than one possible outcome to the encounter.

Wonder—The encounter can in some way be more satisfying than you had imagined. (In which case a sense of wonder is aroused.)

Humor—The encounter can twist away from your expectations in a way that is neither wondrous nor terrible. (In which case a laugh is usually evoked.)

Horror—The encounter can be more painful or traumatizing than you had imagined possible. (In which case terror or horror are aroused.)

Because of this, young readers, by virtue of age alone, are biologically predisposed to be drawn to works of wonder (fantasy or science fiction), humor, and horror. Those are the largest draws for them.

Statistically, those are the strongest draws. How strong are they? Ninety-eight percent of children are drawn to wonder. Ninety-six percent are drawn to humor. Ninety-two percent to horror.

As a child reaches puberty, testosterone leads boys to become more combative and competitive than the girls. Hence, young men begin becoming attracted to adventure by the age of five or six, and by the late teens it becomes a primary draw. Sexual interest (pornographic element) also become a powerful emotional draw, reaching the height of its power during the middle- and late teens.

Young women on the other hand begin to develop a strong interest in romance just before puberty, at the age of eleven through thirteen. Sure, the young women may be interested in having their romances placed in fantastic settings—witness the popularity of *Pirates of the Caribbean*—but the romance and sexual angles are as important as the fantasy.

By the mid-20s, the draw for fantastic literature is no longer overwhelming, and people in that age range may quit reading fantastic literature and watching fantasy films altogether. Men may begin picking up thrillers instead of science fiction, while women lean toward straight contemporary romances.

As your audience ages, the sexual draws gradually stop interesting the readers at all. In part, it's because of the failing hormone levels in adults. A woman at 40 is nearing menopause, and the male at 50 is reaching a hormonal crisis of his own. They lose interest in sex to a great degree. Instead, adults who are raising their own children are confronted with myriad problems—how do I teach my child to get along with others? Why doesn't my husband ask for directions when he gets lost? And so on. Older readers tend to be more thoughtful, more grounded in reality, and more interested in stories that have practical applications to their own lives.

Older women tend to become more interested in mysteries and dramas as they reach their 40s, and men's taste in fiction soon follows.

Thus, as you begin to try to categorize your audience, you can see that the emotional draws to your story—wonder, humor, horror, adventure, romance, mystery, suspense, and drama—need to appeal to your target audience.

You want to write a story that doesn't have a hope of success? Try aiming a contemporary family drama at six-year-olds. From an audience analysis it sounds silly. Yet it happens all of the time. A 50-year-old grandmother decides that she wants to write a children's book, and what does she write: a story about a kid who has to try to save the farm from ruin during the Great Depression. She loves drama, so she writes drama—completely unaware as to why children stay away from her book in droves.

Less than 10% of children respond to drama as a draw.

In the same way, wonder literature for the over-60 crowd tends to win few fans, too.

Some emotional appeals can even drive an audience away. For example, let's say that you try to create a pornographic movie aimed at young women. About 85% of them will report that they react negatively to your story, while a very few might respond positively.

If you want to succeed, pay attention to what the most powerful emotional draws are for your audience age, and cater to their tastes.

Here are some of the emotional draws that are important to you:

Very young children—ages 0-5: Like wonder and humor in that order. Note that spooky stories may attract them, but can easily terrify a toddler. Mysteries can also attract a little one.

Children—ages 6-11: Wonder, humor and horror are the top three attractions, with adventure beginning to draw young men. A great example of what you're trying to accomplish can be seen in R.L. Stine's *Goosebump* series.

Girls—Age 11-19: Wonder, humor, and horror are still important, but by age 13-16 romance becomes the primary draw. Also, note that this is the time when girls will become more interested in coming of age stories. They're trying to understand the world and cope with their own growing powers, and they're trying to understand their place in society.

Boys—Age 11-19: Wonder, humor, and horror are still important, but by age 11 adventure becomes a primary draw for young men, so they may find themselves enticed by stories set in football camps or on road trips. By age 16, young men also will be more drawn to sexual content.

Women—Age 20-40: By age 20, women are drawn primarily to romance, but they also enjoy humor, and horror, mystery and some drama. As they age, the interest in romance declines, and drama and mystery become much stronger draws.

Men—Age 20-50: By age 20, men are drawn primarily to adventure, and this remains the strongest draw until about age 50. As men age, they too become more engaged by dramas and mysteries, leaving behind the wonder literature that they enjoyed in their youth.

So human predilections toward certain emotional draws at given ages are a valuable indicator of how well stories will perform in the market. In Hollywood, advertising firms can predict how well a film will do simply by taking a look at a commercial, counting the number and types of each emotional beat (an emotional beat is a scene or sound effect that promises to play upon a certain emotion), multiplying that number by the percentage of audience members who are drawn to each of the given types of emotional beats, and multiplying that by the "reach" of the film (a measurement of how many times a given commercial is likely to be viewed by potential audience members). When all is said, a raw score is used as a comparative to other movies, and based on such comparisons, marketing firms are able to guess within about five percentage points how well a film will do during its first two opening weeks.

Now, here is something important. In Hollywood, we studied a number of emotional tags—wonder, humor, horror, drama, mystery, romance, pornography—but we didn't study all of the emotions. For example, a story that creates a strong sense of nostalgia can be very popular, but we never measured that. A story that creates a strong sense of hope is also powerful, but we never measured that. In *Lord of the Rings,* Tolkien played upon a strong sense of loss to good effect. In other words, as you consider imbuing your work with an emotional tone, feel free to use emotions that haven't been used in our examples.

With novels, we don't do marketing research to the same degree that we do with film. We don't have the kind of money that it takes to run a Hollywood-style "greenlight analysis" on a novel in order to figure out whether our books will draw a huge audience. But as novelists, we really should know how to greenlight our own stories.

Taking Steps to Expand Your Audience

I took a lot of writing classes in college, and I think that in just about every one I took, the professor pointed out that the world is made up of both men and women, but beginning writers typically only write stories for people of their own sex. That's because they are used to reading stories primarily about people of their own sex.

But think about it: why would you want write to a small audience?

So let's say that you're a male, writing a story aimed primarily at men. Currently the earth has some 7,000,000,000 people in it. Of those people, over half are women.

It only makes economic sense that if you could capture readers of both sexes, you would more than double your income.

Of course, not all authors want to capture readers of both sexes. There are men who are only interested in writing for other men. Women are too hard to understand, they think, and as a male author you may be afraid that you won't be able to write about them convincingly.

Similarly, some women don't feel that they can write stories that will engage men.

So we tend to write stories about people who are of our same sex, and roughly our same age.

Some authors take it much further. I happen to be a Mormon. I know lots of Mormons who are so deeply rooted in their own culture, that they couldn't write authentically about someone who was an atheist, a Catholic, or a Muslim. So these authors tend to write for the 15 million people who belong to their church. But with such a small audience to draw from, very few of them can make a living.

And that's the crux of the problem: the smaller the audience you write for, the tougher it is to support your writing habit. If you want to write a novel that could only really be appreciated by Texans, you've got a fairly small audience. You want to narrow it further and say it's just for men. The audience gets smaller still. You want to decide that it's only for men who like polyester, and it shrinks further.

So I suggest that you look for ways to expand your audience rather than minimize it. Here are a couple of authors who did just that. Let's take J. K. Rowling first.

In chapter one of *Harry Potter*, three people gather together to leave a child on the doorstep of a *muggle* family. One is the aging headmaster of a school for wizards. The second is a woman of similar age, and the third is middle-aged giant. Though young Harry Potter himself is only a babe, he takes the center stage not because he's the viewpoint character, but because:

—He's the one that the others are talking about

—He is so powerful even as a baby, that he has just killed a Dark Lord.

Do you see what Rowling has done? She has inhabited her scene with people of diverse backgrounds, from newborn babes to graybeards, both male and female. The group is small enough to be intimate, large enough to give us diversity.

She then continues with this throughout the books. Harry grows up in a nasty household, is rescued by wizards, and soon meets a nice cast of friends and enemies—once again of varying ages and sexes.

The reason for this should be obvious, but in case it is not, here it goes: the easiest way to engage a member of a particular demographic is to write about a character in that demographic so that the reader can develop a rooting interest in that character. Of course, the easiest way to gain rooting interest is to show that this person is somehow like the reader.

In short, we almost always grow attached to people who are like us. Women tend to feel more strongly for other women—women who are their age or slightly younger. It's easier to empathize with such characters. And of course men tend to empathize with other men.

In fact, some 30 percent of men say that they can't enjoy books about women. Not that they "don't" enjoy them, they can't empathize with the protagonists at all. Similarly, about ten percent of women can't empathize with men.

Young readers not only can't empathize with the very old, some studies show that the lines and creases on an old person's face can easily be misread to the point that an old woman smiling at a child can be seen, from the point of view of the child, as an old person interested in devouring the child.

Not only that, we tend to empathize with people of our own nationality. Once again, Rowling populates her story with people from diverse cultures, having tournaments where the English people interact with those from other nations. You'll meet people from Ireland, France, Soviet Bloc countries, Asia, and India in her stories.

In short, as an author she learned early on to try to capture wide demographics—both male and female, old and young.

Here's another writer who learned to maximize his audience: James Cameron. I recall back in 1993 watching the movie *Titanic* for the first time. Cameron doesn't cater particularly to children, but he did do something interesting. In populating his ship, he shows immigrants crossing the oceans from dozens of nations—France, Spain, Germany, Italy, India, China, and so on. He makes it a massive multicultural event. As an English speaker, you might not notice what he did. After all, each of these families that are shown get only a few seconds of screen time. Sometimes, they are simply heard and seen in passing. Yet we see them, we hear them, and their stories get woven into the fabric of a greater tale.

As I watched what Cameron did, I was impressed at how gracefully he braided these stories together. I recall thinking, "He's going to set international sales records with this. I wonder if the studios know it?" Of course, he did know it. In fact, he did something unprecedented with the movie: he released it all across the world, translated into dozens of languages, all on the same day.

The result was that *Titanic* doubled the sales of the next bestselling movie of all time.

It didn't take much work on Cameron's part. He simply populated his story with people from dozens of countries. In fact, if you will sit down and watch it, you'll note something interesting. The largest sales territories for selling movies at the time were: the United States, England, Germany, France, Italy, Spain, Japan, and Australia—pretty much in that order. If you watch the movie and count, you'll notice that actors from all of those nations are present in the movie. In short, Cameron wove them into the film in order to guarantee good distribution in those countries.

Now, I have to admit, that I've sometimes done the same. I do it subtly sometimes, but I do it. If you read *The Runelords*, you'll note that I have characters with English and Scottish names, mostly, but among the royalty we have people like Gaborn Val Orden—a German name—which is very important. I also use Iome, a French name, or Ahten, an Egyptian name. If you pay attention to accents and sentence structures, you'll see that characters' voices often hark back to their roots.

But I don't just weave multiculturalism into a few names, I weave it into the very fabric of the story. For example, I have one powerful subplot dealing with Sir Borenson, a man whose honor is tested to the core in a very oriental way. I wrote it hoping to appeal to a Japanese and Chinese audience. Ten years ago, I was invited to China to see about making the book into a movie. In that visit, I was introduced to one of China's foremost producers—their Steven Spielberg, so to speak. He had my screenplay translated into Chinese before my visit, and so he had a chance to read the story. When we met that morning, he politely bowed – a custom that is not commonly practiced in China since the Cultural Revolution. As he bowed, dozens of businessmen fell back in astonishment and gasped. You see, he had a reputation for being a very proud man. When receiving China's highest honors for artistic achievement, he refused to bow to the premiere on national television. So the notion that this man who would bow to no one would bow to me … well, it dropped a few jaws.

So I asked him why he bowed. His answer was simple. "No Western writer has ever understood the heart of the Asian as you do. This movie will be the most popular American film ever to hit China—far bigger than *Star Wars*, far bigger than *Jurassic Park*." I was delighted to hear it. I'd spent months studying the concepts of honor—giri and gimu—as taught by the Japanese. I quite frankly find myself very much attracted to their code. So I was happy to see how deeply the story had touched him.

As a result of this bow, something odd happened. Within four hours, the script for the movie was rushed through China's censorship board and approved not only for filming in China but for distribution. Normally, this process would have taken years. It normally took two years to get a script approved for filming, and then once the film was made, it could take another nine months for approval. But based upon one director's estimation of the story, we made history. So one key to enlarging your audience is to create a diverse cast of characters.

Climbing the Emotional Richter Scale

Bestsellers register high on the emotional-Richter scale.

Now, there is nothing wrong in writing stories that don't adhere to a formula. You can do just fine writing mystery novels set in the present day that feature an old woman as a protagonist, for example. It has been done with some success before. The audience is wide enough so that you can make a living at it.

There's nothing set in stone that says that you have to set your books in another time and place in order to sell. Contemporary stories for teens can work well.

You can also decide that you're only interested in writing to teenage girls rather than have a broad audience, ala Stephenie Meyer.

But here's something interesting. You can't ignore one thing: you still have to score high on the emotional Richter scale if you want to create a bestseller.

Some authors will say, "Well I don't want to appeal to my readers' emotions, I want to appeal to their intellect." But when you appeal to a reader's intellect—when you surprise them with insights, or make them feel as if their head will explode from a revelation, or when you twist your story in dizzying directions that they'd never imagined—your intellectual insights invariably lead to powerful emotional responses.

So you have to carefully consider each scene and ask yourself questions like, "What is the emotional draw behind this scene?" If it's drama, and I'm writing a romance, how well will my reader respond? If I tell a joke, is it a good joke, one that really keeps the reader laughing, maybe even days later? Or in my comedy, are there enough humorous notes. We've all been lured to movies that are advertised as comedies and then found that all three of the good jokes we saw in the commercials are the only ones used in what is otherwise a drama. We felt cheated.

So how well does your story stack up to others in its genre? If you're writing horror, how strong are your horror beats? Will you surpass films like *Jaws, The Shining,* and *Aliens?*

You may also find that your story can be strengthened if you add entire new dimensions. For example, let's say that you're writing a comedy. Will it help you get your 20-something audience if you add a romance line? Or what happens if you create a bit of adventure?

When you look for ways to expand your audience, you'll find that you make surprising and valuable changes to your story.

PULLING IT ALL TOGETHER

For the past 30,000 words I've been discussing some of the basics of audience analysis. Hopefully by now you recognize a few truths:

First, telling stories can be a very healthy activity. Through it, your audience can be entertained, emotionally strengthened, educated, and can grow through shared experiences. Stories bind communities together and can help create a consensus about how we should act and feel.

So as you create your stories, you need to consider what it is that your audience wants and needs. That should be a huge priority in your mind.

We can show that audiences of certain ages and sexes will crave slightly different things—wonder, humor, horror, romance, adventure, intrigue, drama.

And we also know that by studying what has been popular in the past, we can gain some insights into how to create powerful stories for the future.

Don't restrict yourself to any one medium. If you want to write a powerful novel, you can draw inspiration outside books. One of the most popular books in years was *The Hunger Games*. Author Suzanne Collins reported that the idea came as she was switching between two channels on television. One of the channels had footage from the war in Iraq, and it became juxtaposed over a popular reality television show—and combined to create a runaway bestselling book!

So as a storyteller, you draw your inspiration from wherever you can find it.

SECTION 2

IDENTIFY THE ELEMENTS THAT HELP YOU PLOT YOUR STORY

In this section, we will study what the parts of a story are so that you will understand what you need to do in order to create a fulfilling tale.

ELEMENTS OF A STORY

As I've said before, there are several elements to a story. Orson Scott Card has said that a story can be guided by milieu, idea, character, and event. (See his book *Characters and Viewpoint*).

I prefer to think that other things help guide your story. Certainly milieu, idea, character and *emotion* might seem like better tags to me. After all, we divide our literary genres by the emotion that they evoke. When you go to the bookstore, you'll see sections for romance, thrillers, horror, adventure, wonder (usually called speculative fiction or science fiction and fantasy), humor, and so on. So there are a number of ways to think about story elements, and I'll go into more depth of these later.

For our purposes here, I'm going to divide our story into four aspects:

—*Milieu*: The setting of your story includes the time and place that the story occurs, even if it is only an imaginary setting. The milieu is perhaps where most stories need to begin, simply because the milieu so strongly defines the types of characters that you may have, the society that they live in, and so on.

—*Character*: The characters of your story grow out of their milieu, to some degree, but the characters also generate your conflicts. In short, it's the conflicts between and within your characters that create the plot. So we'll talk about how to create characters in a bit more depth.

—*Conflicts*: The conflicts between the characters, and of course the way that characters struggle to resolve those conflicts, really define your plot. You need to consider how your conflicts arise, how they build relentlessly, and how they are resolved in your story. As an author you'll spend a good amount of time just thinking about little things, such as "Why is it that my protagonist doesn't just run away? What's his motivation?" or "Would my character really do that?" or "How can I make this ending climax more powerful?"So we're going to talk about plots and plotting devices.

—*Treatment*: Beyond the things mentioned above, you as a writer bring your own special talents to a work. A strong and intriguing voice might draw readers, or your smooth handling of tone, or your skills at describing events, or your lyrical style. In short, your unique writing skills can often turn a drab story into something engrossing, and, in fact, most editors and agents will evaluate a manuscript initially based almost on your treatment alone. So it becomes important to develop strong writing skills. Teaching these basic writing skills goes beyond the scope of this book.

BRAINSTORMING
YOUR SETTINGS

The milieu of your story consists of the setting—both its time and its place. Thus we might have a story set in London in 1898, or in Montana seventy million years ago, or in the town of Hobbiton during the Great War.

In mainstream literature, we typically deal with settings that either already exist or that have existed historically. Thus, when you write about the city of Chicago, it behooves you to do your research. If you say that there is a great sandwich shop on the corner of 25th and Regal, there had better be one there, lest your reader (who happens to live on that corner) recognizes that you don't know what you're talking about.

So the great skill that you need to develop in order to create a setting for a contemporary or historical novel is to do research on your setting, and then figure out how to incorporate that research into a story.

However, if your city is made up—for example Soap Opera, Georgia—your audience will take it for granted that the city is something of your own creation.

Whether you're using a real setting or making one up, though, you need to understand that not all settings are created equal. Not all settings will draw the same number of readers.

The Power of Transport

I mentioned that if you look at the bestselling movies of all time, you would find they have one element in common: they all transport you to another time and place. The same trend can be seen in novels.

The super-agent Albert Zuckerman, in his book *Writing the Blockbuster Novel*, suggests that in choosing your settings you should choose (or in the case of speculative fiction writers create) a setting that doesn't just transport an audience but transports them to a place that they would like to be.

Thus he would advise you that rather than have a scene set in Boise, Idaho, you should see if you can move it someplace more exotic and desirable, such as Paris or Monaco. In particular, he believes that folks are curious about the lavish lifestyles of the upper-crust. People would like to be transported to posh resorts and the halls of power.

To some degree he's right. Television shows like *Lifestyles of the Rich and Famous* and *The Bachelor* cater to such tastes, as do many a spy novel and romance.

And as if to verify this notion, there are some settings that almost always spell doom for a film—prisons, tenement houses, ghettos.

Yet sometimes people can be fascinated by truly vile settings. Take a look at the *Alien* movies. The planet where the aliens are found is a nasty place—hazy, dirty, and constantly raining, while the local predators are shocking in their nastiness. Yet people not only watched the first movie, they hungered for further installments.

There are lots of examples of harsh or nasty places that people like to visit in speculative fiction. I hate hot weather and I know that I'd wither and die on the planet Dune, but I've traveled there in my imagination many times. Have you ever noticed how harsh life sounds on Pern? Everyone is scrambling for their next meal. It doesn't sound like a particularly appealing place. I could go on and on.

In most of these cases, the settings often have some particularly powerful draw that offsets the negatives.

For example, in Anne McCaffrey's *Pern* novels you not only get to ride the dragons, you get to bond with them on an almost spiritual level—you get to find a life-mate. On Arrakis the desert is deadly, but the draw is Melange—which lets you tap into your ancestral memories and bestows upon many the gift of prophecy. Tolkien's world can also be a nasty place— with its forests of giant spiders and tunnels filled with orcs and trolls, but the horrors are balanced by the ethereal beauty of the elves, the nobility of the humans, the admirable stoutness of the dwarves, and the childlike innocence of the hobbits.

Each of these settings has one thing in common: each of them is deeply intriguing. Each is loaded with curiosities and mysteries.

In short, in creating your fantasy or science fiction world, *arousing a sense of wonder* might well be your primary goal. As you create that sense of wonder – by subjecting your characters to places, people, and creatures that truly are unique – you might also carefully consider your world. Ask yourself, does the beauty balance the horror? Does the darkness overwhelm the light? Will my readers want to visit here, or will they want to flee? Will they want to return to the land that I create, time and time again?

It isn't just enough to create a setting. As writers, our goal should be, from time to time, to create a place where weary readers will seek rest from their journeys.

Dealing with Repetitive Settings

The rule of thumb in Hollywood for big-budget movies says, "Don't show me the same setting twice." Thus, if you have a mobster meet your hero at a strip club in scene one, you don't want to repeat that location. The reason is that you want to keep the story visually interesting by making sure that each scene shows the viewer something new.

This rule is pretty hard and fast for big-budget films, but not for films with a smaller budget. For example, in the movie *My Dinner with Andre*, the entire is shot on one set. And of course in low-budget movies, a producer might really enjoy the savings that come with having three scenes shot in the same location. But you should be aware that if you're writing a book that you hope will be adapted to film, it is likely that scenes set in the same location will be rewritten into new locations. Perhaps you might want to consider saving your screenwriter some work—and looking like a genius at the same time.

A second rule of screenwriting that applies here is: make it interesting. For example, if you set a scene in a house, it shouldn't be a generic "indoor house." People go to movies to see something new. Make it a place they haven't been before. For example, let's say that I'm setting a novel in Australia. I could describe a "lonely farmhouse" somewhere, but it would be like farmhouses around the world. But in Coober Pedy, Australia, folks often dig their homes underground to escape the harsh heat. At the same time, they will be mining opals as they "dig themselves a new bedroom." If I were going to set a tale in Australia, I might consider such a location just because it would be interesting, different. But why not do something unique with multiple settings, look for challenging new places to start your tale?

When I'm judging for Writers of the Future, reading the slush piles, I can't tell you how many fantasy stories I read that open with the heroes sitting in the common room of an inn. I get to the point where I want to reject them out of hand.

One way to make any indoor house scene unique, of course, is to build or furnish it to the tastes of the owner. Thus, an avid fisherman might have a fly-tying room, while a woman who loves to make pots might have a kitchen table covered with green ware.

There is one other good reason to vary even your exterior settings. Let's say you are writing an "epic." There are a number of strategies for writing these, whether they be adventures, fantasies, or whatnot. The point of an epic is to give the reader of your story the feeling that he has lived a whole life, traveled the world.

Now, Chaucer tried to create an epic by writing about citizens of a village—the nobility, the peasants, the workmen—and creating a sense of wholeness that way. Some Russian authors believed that a proper epic needed to capture all of the various levels of language—lord to pauper, husband to wife, father to child—in order to convey an epic sense.

But I would say that in creating an epic fantasy, in devising a whole world, we would want to create one that explores various lands, oceans, and climes in order to give the reader that we as authors have truly formed a whole new universe. Such a universe, of course, would not be a static thing. It would include a mythic and historic past, and it would seem to be rushing toward some intriguing future.

Over the years, in reading tales from new authors, I've been surprised by how often I find that writers will neglect to give us any sense of setting in their story. In particular, authors trained primarily as screenwriters often feel that a single line of description—something not much longer than "interior of house, night"—serves to create a setting. Writers who fail in this respect once seem to do it over and over, as a matter of habit.

It's important for you as a writer to remember this: if you study the bestselling movies of all time, you'll find that all of them transport the viewer to another place time. Whether we're talking about *The Passion of Christ, The Titanic, Star Wars, Harry Potter, Jurassic Park, The Godfather*, or any of the others, this rule holds true.

So as a writer, your success will be determined largely by your ability to transport a reader to another place and time.

Half-hearted attempts at creating a setting just don't cut it. Don't make that mistake—ever! Don't let your imagination fail you in this step of the creation process.

In brainstorming any setting for any story, it's important to remember that settings aren't static. By that I mean that a setting isn't just a place that you put your character, like an empty room with nothing but a chair. The setting should have an impact on the character, and the character will often have an impact on the setting.

A setting is a place that should exist in your mind, that should have a life of its own outside of the character. The setting should interact with your character, and vice versa.

When You Imagine Your Setting, Try a Couple of Tricks

First, in every scene, the setting should impinge upon the character's senses. For example, imagine you have two characters talking in the woods as they walk along. Ask yourself, "how could the setting impinge upon the character?" One way might be through the aural senses. Your characters might be startled by the bark of a squirrel as it scurries up a tree, or the sound of a twig snapping in the distance as a hart bounds away. Or maybe the setting impinges visually as a bird goes winging through a slanting beam of sunlight, or tree-tops that are blowing in the wind cause the slants of sunlight to move and dance. Or perhaps the setting will impinge upon the character through smell, as your character notices the scent of some bitter weeds or an old campfire or the scent of bear dung as he passes a spot. Or it might impinge through the sense of touch—as your character finds it suddenly cold as he moves into the shadows of the deeper woods. We might even have some physical impact. Perhaps your characters find that they must struggle over a fallen log, or wade through a bog.

Second, as you're creating your setting, think of how your setting may impact the plot as your character interacts with it. In the woods above for example, you might imagine the different ways that the woods might impinge upon your character's journey. If you've ever tried traipsing through real virgin wilderness, you know that it isn't easy. In some places, thick bushes might cover the forest floor to a height of a dozen feet or more. Ever tried walking through sword tail ferns or Oregon grape that rise up to your chest? It can't be done quietly. And you're constantly trying to negotiate wind-fallen trees, uneven ground, and so on. Then of course there are the pests—biting flies, midges, bees, and so on, not to mention the fact that the weather always has a mind of its own, and may rain on you relentlessly one moment and then seem to decide to freeze the next for no reason other than to annoy you. So maybe your characters have to stop beneath the shelter of a tree for a moment to put on warmer jackets—or to shed those jackets later as they begin to sweat from strenuous exercise.

Third, as you create your setting, try not to think of it as something that is stagnant. Give your setting a history, and a future. As you create a castle, for example, you might consider what wall and defenses were added or changed over the life of the building. A castle typically is born as a small fort or manor house, and as its value as a retreat is recognized, new towers and walls might pop up every hundred years or so, until after a thousand years it might be imposing indeed. Or perhaps some other fortress gains import in its stead, and so it dies—becoming nothing but the bones of a castle, left scattered upon some hill.

When you create any building, hill, river or tree, consider where that object lies upon the timeline of its life. Consider not only what it has been, but what it will soon become. By giving your setting a life of its own, you will go a long way toward convincing your reader that your story has a life of its own.

BUILDING CHARACTERS

Dozens of books can tell you how to create characters, and so I won't spend a lot of time on it here. One text that I recommend is *Building Believable Characters* by Marc McCutcheon. In it, he will guide you through the process of creating characters that have multiple dimensions—dealing with external traits, personality disorders, the kinds of clothes they wear, habits and opinions, medical histories, and so on.

If you're a new author, I recommend such a book simply because most authors have one or two blind spots in their characterization. For example, when I was young, I wrote my first novel, and my editor called up and asked, "What is your heroine wearing on page 186?" I thought a moment and answered, "Clothes."

As a new writer, I didn't care much about what my characters were wearing. Frankly, as those who have observed my closet first-hand can tell you, I don't care much about *my own* wardrobe, so why would I spend time making up clothes for imaginary people?

I've seen new authors who create a cast of characters, and not one of them seems to have a personal relationship outside the novel. That's a blind spot. I've seen authors who write all characters with the same voice. I once read a story by an author who described the love interest as "the woman with the big tits" for the first five pages. (I quit reading after that, though a morbid sense of curiosity makes me wonder to this day if she ever got a name, a hair color, or any hint of a personality. Only the absurdity of the author's approach got me five pages into the story in the first place.)

But I have to admit that all of this cataloguing of traits might be fairly worthless. I can't see spending 80 pages to create a character's background for a normal novel. It's overkill.

An approach I have found to be far more valuable is one that I haven't seen taught anywhere else. The basic idea is this: stories aren't about characters so much as they are about growth. In other words, your characters will change and grow throughout a novel, and it isn't necessarily the character herself that is interesting, but that process of change.

So when I'm generating characters, I often find that I can kick-start a whole story by composing a character that is going to go through a change. Here are a couple of samples:

Sister Mary Teresa had never wanted to make love to a man until she met Father McFarland, and in that instant she repented of her vow chastity and silently began to plan an affair.

It had only been three days since last I'd seen Sir Fader, yet immediately I knew that something was terribly wrong, for in that time his hair had turned from burnished red to snowy white, and there was a haunted look in his eyes that made me stumble away in fear when he glanced at me.

You can of course think of your own little hooks for introducing a character. If you're writing a story, consider the growth or changes that your character will be required to go through, and then compose a sentence or two describing that moment when your character changes from what he was to what he will be. Eventually, that moment will become a pivotal scene.

For example, in heroic fiction, there is an archetypal moment that occurs when a young man or woman sets aside their fears and decides to risk everything to become a hero. Often, that moment follows the death of a loved one—a father or wife. At the very least, it will usually involve the hero witnessing some terrible injustice.

In the same way, you'll find that villains need to grow. Many writers make the mistake of trying to create villains who are stagnant. They are bad simply because they are evil. But a far more interesting villain is one who is faced with moral choices, who struggles with them, and does not always do what is evil. He sometimes shows mercy. He sometimes is benevolent. But in the end, when faced with his biggest challenge of all, he falls. In other words, your story should not start with a villain, but should grow a villain.

You'll find that when you enjoy a story immensely, there is almost always some character growth. One of my favorite movies in recent years was *As Good as it Gets*, with Jack Nicholson. In it, Jack is a horrible man—a smug novelist who is so neurotic that he can hardly step out of his own apartment. He's both a homophobe and misogynist, and so he is a terribly lonely man. But during the course of the film, he grows tremendously, winning the love of a good woman and finally taking in the gay man next door as a roommate. In the film, each character experiences a life-altering moment that makes them more accepting of others, more loving, and ultimately more human than they had been before.

For each of your characters, you would be wise to look at them and not worry so much about how many nose hairs they have or what their social security number is, but to consider what kind of growth that character might experience in your tales.

Creating Character Growth by Building Between Stages of Life

In fact, one way to create a good character arc is to look at what your character is, and then consider how to move them to the next state of existence. For example, in the movie *Gladiator*, we open with a character who is a powerful general. He is accused of being a traitor, and then sold as a slave. In order to escape a life of servitude, he quickly becomes a gladiator, and there has the opportunity to either regain his freedom or gain vengeance. Do you see how the character arc works?

In LeCarre's novel *Tinker, Tailor, Soldier, Spy* we see a character journey in the very title.

In a typical hero journey story, the protagonist often starts as an orphan. He then goes out into a new world and becomes a wanderer, meeting new people. As he witnesses terrible injustice, he becomes a warrior, until the time when he recognizes that he must become a martyr and risk everything for his newfound society.

So give it a try. Map out your character's growth arc in order to generate ideas for your story.

Populating Your Tale

It's almost never enough to create a single character for your tale. As you prepare an outline, you might have dozens of characters that are needed to fill out your story. So populating your tale may become an intimidating activity.

Years ago, I studied how Shakespeare would create characters. In each of his plays, a mortal and intellectual battle was taking place, and various characters would be called upon to voice various sides of the argument.

I diagrammed his method of character casting out many years ago, but others have done it more recently at a site called dramatica.com. I'm going to present here, briefly, a hybrid discussion on how to populate a tale based upon my own research and the work of the folks at Dramatica.

Basically, the idea here is that you learn to think of a story on the basis of "roles" that need to be filled. Sometimes, two or three characters may perform the same roles, and that is okay. So let's talk about some of the roles you may need to fill.

The Protagonist

At the heart of your tale is a protagonist—someone who wants to do right, but is often torn in his feelings. For example, he might want to be a good soldier and be compassionate toward his enemies at the same time. This duality in your protagonist is absolutely necessary if you're to gain power from internal conflicts.

Examples from popular films include people like Luke Skywalker in *Star Wars*, Frodo Baggins in *Lord of the Rings*, and Harry Potter in *Harry Potter*.

The Antagonist

The antagonist is normally a person who wants to coerce your character to follow a life path that is soul-destroying, even though he may gain some short-term goal. Antagonists are usually older and far more powerful than the protagonist. The antagonist in the above movies are the emperor in Star Wars, the Dark Lord Sauron in *The Lord of the Rings*, and Voldemort in *Harry Potter*.

The Guide

A guide is often a teacher or mentor of some kind, an older person who trains our protagonist. The teaching may include life skills, teaching in how to behave, or it might include military training, martial arts, athletics, and so on. In *Star Wars*, Obi-Wan Kenobi is a guide, while Gandalf performs the same role in *The Lord of the Rings*, and Dumbledore provides the role in *Harry Potter.*

The Contagonist

The contagonist in your story is a powerful character who normally is allied with the antagonist, and is often his most powerful underling.

The contagonist typically sees potential in the protagonist, sees that person as a younger version of himself and will try to become a guide to the protagonist.

Though the contagonist may seem allied to the antagonist, their goals may differ.

In *Star Wars*, the contagonist is Darth Vader. In *The Lord of the Rings*, we have several good contagonists. Gollum is a contagonist for Frodo, but so are the nine Black Riders—and so is Saruman. In *Harry Potter* we see Snape as a possible contagonist throughout the series, but others emerge in the course of individual novels. In particular, in *Goblet of Fire*, we have Professor Moody (who turns out to actually be Death Eater Barty Crouch Jr.) as a contagonist, befriending Harry with the intent to destroy him later on.

The Sidekicks

A young protagonist will typically find people who become allies to him, almost a fan club or a support group.

Luke gets his robots, Han Solo, a Wookie, and a princess. Frodo gets Sam, Merry, Pippin, Legolas, and so on. Harry gets Ron, Hermione, Hagrid, and others.

These people give emotional and physical support when times are darkest, and normally can be depended upon.

However, take warning: one of the sidekicks will almost always betray him. Luke was betrayed by Lando; Frodo was betrayed by Boromir.

The Hecklers/Henchmen

A protagonist will almost always have people who act as hecklers. They will often express a low opinion of the protagonist, and will work in concert with the enemy. Just as the sidekicks give emotional support, the hecklers will often take it away.

At the same time, the hecklers are often in the employ of the antagonist. So they may be enemy combatants or henchmen. They exist to undermine, attack, annoy, harass, and humiliate the protagonist.

In Star Wars, the Imperial Troops are henchmen, as are the bounty hunters and various criminals. In *The Lord of the Rings*, henchmen can be found among various orcs, trolls, goblins, and ghosts.

In *Harry Potter,* we see Crabbe, Goyle, and Malfoy as the primary hecklers, though Voldemort has dozens of henchmen who appear throughout the series.

The Love Interest

A romantic love interest is a combined character. He or she may have some of the intellect of a guide, with some of the dedication of a sidekick. The love interest wants the protagonist to follow a certain course of action, but provides something important—a reward for doing right.

Note that the love interest may also be unsure of the protagonist, and may need to be convinced of the protagonist's true character.

In Star Wars, in episode four Princess Leia was introduced as a possible love interest, but her apparent role was shattered when we later find out that she is Luke's sister. No strong female character was later brought on to inspire Luke to do the right thing, and that perhaps makes him stronger as a character. After all, we shouldn't need strong sexual rewards for doing the right thing.

In *The Lord of the Rings*, Frodo doesn't have a strong love interest either. His love is the Shire, and though he risks everything to save it, in the end it never really does belong to him.

In *Harry Potter*, we secretly root for Hermione as a love interest, but interestingly, once again, that love never matures, though Harry eventually does fall in love.

The Temptress

Just as a true love may help guide and strengthen a character, in classic literature a temptress often appears. This is a person who offers fake love—false assurances, coupled with sex—to the protagonist in order to get him to serve the antagonist.

While the temptress is often personified, just as often it is not. In *Star Wars*, the temptress is the "Dark Side," the easy path to power, wealth, and influence.

In *The Lord of the Rings,* the Ring itself serves as Frodo's temptress, and it nearly destroys him.

In *Harry Potter*, Harry eventually captures a powerful wand that may be seen as his temptress, and like Frodo, he destroys it.

Dealing with a Large Cast of Characters

A reader recently said, "I've taken a bunch of radio dramas that I wrote a few years ago, and I'm trying to combine them into one big story. However, I have a problem: how do I handle a large cast?"

There are real advantages to writing a book with a diverse cast. For one thing, you can attract a wide audience—male, female, old, and young—more easily with a large cast than you can if you're writing to one target audience such as teenage girls. That's why, though Twilight sold remarkably well, it still hasn't ever overtaken Harry Potter. Rowling cast a wider net.

Most large fantasies do the same—things like Game of Thrones and Wheel of Time, but you'll also see this happening with epic historical novels a lot, too, and even with thrillers.

But there are so many pitfalls and drawbacks to writing with a large cast. Will the readers remember who each character is? Will they connect with them? Will they enjoy the whole novel or will they read only one story line and skip the rest?

You want to take advantage of the strengths of having multiple protagonists while avoiding the pitfalls.

So here are some tips for writing stories with a large cast.

Narrow your focus to just a few characters. For a novel, you can really only focus on three or four characters. Each time that you add a new arc for a viewpoint character, the length of your story doubles. This is because each time that you add a new major protagonist, that person now has to have scenes and relationships with all of the others. Literally, the novel doubles the length of the story. (See the book *Story* by Robert McKee for a longer discussion of the phenomenon.)

1. So make an intelligent decision as to who your viewpoint characters are going to be. To a large extent, the age and sex of your protagonists is the single largest factor that determines who your audience will be. If you're going after teens and adults, for example, you want to make your protagonists teens and adults, not children, and not great grandmothers.

Do you just want to pull in a female audience—write a about a female protagonist. If you want a male audience, write about a male. Sure, there are readers who don't care about the sex of the protagonist, but statistically there aren't many.

If you're trying to draw in both males and females, you'll want to have a pretty equal number of protagonists of each sex.

So if you're taking short stories and bringing them together to form one longer work, you may want to look at combining your protagonists from two or three stories into one. For example, let's say that you have one middle-aged protagonist named Jonah Robb in one story, and you have another middle-aged protagonist named Conrad Hegel in another. You might look at the stories and ask yourself, could I rewrite this in such a way so that Jonah and Conrad become the same person?

2. Next, when writing large novels like this, look for ways to cut characters or deemphasize some of them. Consider each character's story arc. Is the little boy in your story really so important that he needs a storyline? Is he really that interesting. Or will your audience be far more interested in the teen girl's arc? The truth is that when you choose to write in a mediocre plot line, you sap the strength of the story that is really driving the book. Don't do it.

3. Next, let the readers know who is important in your story. As authors we tag a character as being important through a number of tactics. Here's a list of them.

A) Viewpoint characters are important. If we bother to write a story from the point of view of a character in chapter one, the reader will expect to follow that character throughout the novel. (I know, I violated that rule in *The Runelords*. I was signaling to the reader that 'this isn't your standard fantasy where everyone will live happily all the way through.)

B) Any character who is given a name is tagged as being important. Thus, if a doorman is given a name, we might expect him to take an important role in your story later on. Otherwise, he should remain just "the doorman."

C) Any character who is powerful becomes important. By that I mean, any character who is powerful enough to change the outcome of a story is important to the reader. Thus a powerful villain is important, but so are resourceful protagonists, characters who act as guides to the protagonists, love interests, sidekicks, contagonists, and so on.

D) Any character who is put into extreme pain, particularly emotional pain, is probably important to the story, simply because he/she is someone that we will feel for.

E) Any character who is extremely likeable, anyone who is struggling to do the right thing, is important, for the same reason as above.

In other words, as you begin telling your story, you can use the above ideas to decide just how important a character will become and whether they are worthy of becoming viewpoint characters in your novel.

As you decide who your cast will be, remember that readers of different ages and different sexes are usually looking or different emotional payoffs. I've written about emotional draws before, but let me put it this way.

Statistically speaking, the strongest draw for a teenage girl is romance. More of them will be drawn to romance than, say, drama or mystery. So when creating that storyline, make sure that you target your readers by focusing on the kind of story that they want. A fifty-year-old woman reading the book may be attracted by mystery and drama, so you might want to have a viewpoint character for her who is involved in intrigue. A teenage boy will be attracted to adventure, so you make sure that his role focuses on that. A middle-grade reader will be interested in wonder, humor, and horror.

So when you're looking at a potential viewpoint character, just ask yourself, "Is this character's story a good fit for my needs?" If not, you either have to change the story or drop that viewpoint.

Of course, just because a character isn't a good fit for a larger arc, that doesn't mean that you need to drop them completely. A minor character who appears for a bit in one novel and then wanders off to live happily ever after can offer some great relief to the reader. It assures them that your series has and end, and that you can write satisfying conclusions.

Once you've decided who your cast will be, you as a writer need to make sure that the reader doesn't forget who each character is. There are several ways to do that.

Make sure that we see the major characters often in your story. One way to do this is to keep your chapters short and have alternating viewpoints. If you go more than forty pages without visiting a character, you've probably ignored them for too long. So that means that if you've got four viewpoint characters and you're alternating chapters, you may want to write short chapters—ten pages each.

You can also keep the characters visible by keeping them together physically. A lot of fantasy writers will have three people meet at an inn, then go off on different quests—only to meet at the end of the novel. This divides your characters, so that you lose focus. There are entire novels where this happens, with Robert Jordan, for example. He may feel that he needs to spend book six in a series with two characters, then spend book seven with two others. So readers who are more interested in the book seven characters are tempted to just skip book six.

So try to keep your focus on a group of characters. Have them talk to each other, or maybe they can talk about or think about characters who aren't on stage in a scene. Their conversation might be as simple as, "Have you heard anything from Alex lately?" just to remind us that we have an Alex storyline. The protagonist might respond, "Yeah, I saw him take a shotgun and head down Washington Street at sunset. Says he's gonna' bag himself a couple of zombies." If you're writing a contemporary piece, you can remind us of a character who falls out of the limelight by having your character text another, read about them on Facebook, and so on.

One way to make a character memorable is to tag each of your characters. By this I mean, you can give each person a distinguishing feature—such as a limp, a red trench coat, or an unusual accent—so that when you bring that person into the story, the reader can quickly identify him or her. When Alex comes limping back from his zombie hunt, a protagonist might have to listen closely to try to determine if that's Alex's limp, or just another cramped-up zombie.

Make sure that each of your protagonists has a gripping story—a complete arc, with his or her own problems and setbacks and grand designs. In order for your story to be memorable, it has to keep the reader intrigued, keep the reader hooked, so that the reader will be excited each time they come to a new segment. Remember that a gripping romance is much different from a gripping adventure or a fascinating mystery. You can have different types of stories woven together into one large tapestry.

Last of all, make sure that you start each scene and end each scene with powerful hooks. When your reader gets to the end of a scene and wonders, "Oh my gosh, how will Alex ever escape the zombies!" The threat needs to be strong enough so that the reader will look forward to it while he reads the following chapter about how Zina has fallen for the incredibly charming zombie lord, and you'll want to keep them reading during the following chapter as Doctor Paulsen tries to determine just what kind of virus it is that has infected mankind and turned them all into zombies in the first place, even as her own daughter sinks further and further under the grip of the plague.

In short, there are some great reasons to write those big sprawling epic novels that weave together the stories of dozens of characters, but you as an author have to work hard to keep your cast manageable, to hook your readers with each of tales, and to make your characters memorable.

Please note that building characters and populating your story is a major chore, one that is worthy of its own book. I'll be putting one out soon!

FINDING THEMES IN YOUR TALE

I mentioned earlier that every story is an argument. Very often, you can find inspiration in plotting your tale by looking at the argument and asking yourself, "What more do I need?"

You will often find that you want or need your characters to behave in certain ways. And as they grow and develop, you may even find that you need to justify why they do what they do. If you get deep enough into their thought processes, you can almost imagine them arguing with you. When that happens, go ahead and find a way to put that argument down on paper, either as internal dialog or in a conversation. It shows that your character is conflicted about something. It often is a point at which a "theme" begins to grow out of your story.

A theme is simply an intellectual argument—played out in the deeds, thoughts, and discussions of your characters—that throws light upon a topic that has real-life implications for your characters.

A famous screenwriting consultant, story doctor, author and producer named Michael Hauge often gives seminars in Hollywood, and I once heard him make an interesting point.

He said that he has never seen a movie or read a book that worked where "the question of the protagonist's identity" doesn't come up. In short, questions like "Who am I?" "What am I?" and "Why am I this way?" are at the core of every great work.

For example, let's say that you have a young hero who meets a woman and falls in love. She has to wonder if that young man would be proper husband material. Her father and mother might look at the young man in question and give numerous and valid reasons as to why he is not. His own tenderness and thoughtfulness toward the young woman might form the nucleus of an argument against the parents' objections. He will of course have to ask himself this question and decide whether to propose. In the end the young woman—and the audience—must make their own decisions.

This whole question of identity seems to lie at the core of every romance that you will ever come across. Because it is so central, the male is often presented as a "mysterious stranger" at first, someone who is reclusive or often called away upon some earth-shattering business—either to consult with royalty or fight in a war.

But as you plot, it might be well to consider:

—What roles must my characters try to fill in this story?

—Do they fit into those roles easily, or do they question themselves?

—Do others question their ability?

—What conflicts will arise because of this?

—What must my character do in order to convince himself, others, and my audience that he or she is fit to assume the roles that they must fulfill?

I'm not going to go as far as Michael Hauge and say that such questions lie at the heart of all great fiction. I can see a couple of ways to get around it. But it is a powerful tool for generating stories.

I'm going to recommend a couple of things for those who are interested in learning more about Michael Hauge's works. He has a DVD out in conjunction with script doctor Christopher Vogler with a little tele-seminar called *The Hero's 2 Journeys*.

Along similar lines, a book that I found valuable in brainstorming years ago was *The Fiction Editor* by Thomas McCormack. It deals heavily with the way that character, setting and theme interact with one another to create what he calls "the somacluster" of a story. I read it about 20 years ago, and still find that I fall back on his ideas from time to time. Thomas was a legendary editor in his day, and my mention of the use of "gads" in creating characterization goes back to him. But I have a word of warning: Thomas's writing is dense with ideas, and when you read him, you will get the most benefit if you consider his work very carefully.

NOVEL PLOTTING TOOLS

A "plotting tool" isn't a physical tool, like a hammer or a screwdriver. Those can be used to help you create better cabinets. Instead, a plotting tool is an idea—one if which applied to a story will *almost* always make it better. However, you will have to be the judge on what plotting tools you will use. After all, it's your story, and you will need to build it to your tastes.

Sometimes a plotting tool is merely a structural suggestion, one that affects the direction a story will go. But since a story grows out of your character, setting, conflicts and themes, sometimes a plotting tool might seem to have as much to do with characterization or theme as it does with structure.

So I'm going to define a plotting tool simply as an idea, any idea, which when added to your story may make it more exciting, interesting, satisfying, or complete.

Given that definition, I've created a list of plotting tools that you might consider using to help flesh out your plots.

Timebombs

There is an old Hitchcock movie that starts with a fellow going into a meeting room and setting a briefcase under a table. The camera cuts away to reveal that inside the briefcase is a bomb set to go off at 5 p.m. The rest of the show continues by simply introducing us to each of the characters who comes into the room, so that we become invested in that character and worry about whether or not that character will live or die.

So this is where I get the plotting device that I call a time-bomb. A timebomb is really just a time limit, a deadline, by which some action in a story must fail or succeed. For example, let's say that you have a character who has always dreamed of buying an island in a river. For years he has been saving up for it, and the widow down the road has said, "When you raise the money, Joe, I'll sell it to you." Well, Joe is getting on in years, and he dreams of building his retirement home there.

Not much tension in that storyline, is there? Joe could go for another 20 years without getting that land. It wouldn't matter. But now we add a timebomb to the story: suddenly the widow dies, and her children must sell the land and split the money. A wealthy movie star offers $2 million for the land, and in order for Joe to realize his dream, he must beat that offer—in cash—and bring the money in within three days. That's a timebomb.

Think about it: a story about a kidnapping wouldn't be much of a story if it didn't have a deadline where the hostage would be killed.

In a fantasy tale, it may be that your hero must perform some deed before some pre-determined event. In romance, it may be that the girl must get her man before she is set to take a job on a cruise ship that is leaving to Jamaica.

Whatever your timebomb, make sure that the time limit seems realistic, that it puts extreme stress on the characters, and that the consequences of failing to meet the deadline are devastating.

Dilemma

One of the most powerful plotting devices is to present your protagonist with a dilemma. A dilemma occurs when the protagonist is presented with two equally displeasing choices.

In *The Runelords*, I made use of this to good effect in my magic system. A powerful king, Raj Ahten, is able to drain attributes from his subjects. He has drained the "wit," the ability to store information, from Iome's father, King Sylvarresta. So long as Sylvarresta lives, Raj Ahten is a greater threat to all those around him. But if he is killed, then Raj Ahten will be weakened.

A moral dilemma arises because Sylvarresta's best friend, King Orden, realizes that he must order the executions of anyone who has given use of his attributes to Raj Ahten— including King Sylvarresta. King Orden orders the execution, and spends a great deal of time trying to justify his actions to his family and subjects, but of course Orden finds that there is no course of action that he can win.

In every story, your character will be faced with multiple problems. In some sort of an inciting incident, your character will actually recognize that a major life-changing event has occurred, and he will try to figure out how to overcome that problem. As he does so, he will find that the problem is more challenging than he first thought. In other words, his first attempts to resolve the problem will fail, and he will be forced to devote greater and greater energy to resolving that problem throughout the course of the story. At the very minimum, he must attempt to resolve the problem on three separate occasions.

Thus, if you look at a tightly plotted movie like The *Terminator*, you will notice that there are three major scenes where the terminator goes hunting for his prey, and as he gets closer, the protagonists must work harder and harder to evade him.

Now, when using a dilemma, it is often best to have the dilemma arise early in the story—upon the first or second attempt to resolve the problem. This way, it gives your audience more time to deal with the consequences of an act.

Crucibles

When we talk about writing, there are three kinds of crucibles—crucibles of setting, relationship, or condition. We'll talk about those in a moment, but first we need to define, "What is a *crucible.*"

In metalsmithing, a crucible is a container used to hold metal or liquid as it boils. For example, to melt gold, one takes a heavy bowl made from steel and sets it in a fire. The steel, which can withstand higher temperatures than gold, doesn't melt. But the small container quickly becomes super-heated, so that the gold liquefies in moments.

In fiction, a crucible is any setting, condition, or relationship that keeps characters (such as a protagonist and an antagonist) from splitting apart.

By forcing these characters to remains together, we may sometimes create an almost intolerable atmosphere. It allows us to super-charge the relationships, raise the heat.

For example, imagine that John and Mary have been married for years, but have grown apart. They decide that they don't love each other anymore. The logical thing for them to do would be to divorce and split up, right?

But there's no story in that! The characters could easily resolve the situation by leaving—so as a writer you need them to stay together.

So imagine that John and Mary have grown apart, but both love their six-month-old daughter. Neither is willing to end the relationship so long as they risk losing the child. Now you have a crucible, a binding force that keeps the two together.

But there are different kinds of crucibles. Maybe it is a child. But maybe you could do the same by putting them both in a car and having them get stuck in a snowstorm. The car is a different kind of container from the relationship, but both work to keep the couple together.

So here are the three different types of crucibles.

Crucibles of Setting

A setting may act as a crucible. You've all seen comedies where several people are stuck in a cabin in a snowstorm, and each of them is at the other's throat. You will also quickly remember stories about people on airplanes or trains together. A crucible of setting might be a story set in your characters' workplace, on a ship, or in a small town. In *The Lord of the Rings*, those who had joined the Fellowship were thrust into a crucible—a small band of men forced to band together for their own protection.

The important point is to keep the characters together as much as possible, and to let personalities rub against one another until their tempers boil.

Crucibles of Relationship

You can never escape your family. You might try, but often the family relationship is a crucible. A child wanting to leave home is in a crucible in the same way that a father who must pay child-support is in a crucible. Any two people who are married are in a crucible, as are any two people who happen to just be in love.

I recall a fine western when I was young about two heroic cowboys who are both in love with the same woman. They are forced to band together to rescue her from a kidnapper. The men hate each other, and as the audience gets to know each man better, they both come to vie for our affections.

Soldiers in a squadron will find themselves in a crucible. It may be that you find yourself fighting beside someone you detest—a murderer or a rapist—and yet you are unable to just walk away from the conflict.

A crucible may also be your conflict with your culture. We've probably all known various folks—Catholics, Jews, Muslims, etc., who try to leave their religion behind but can never stop talking about it. But it doesn't have to be your religious culture. My father ran away from the Blue Ridge Mountains to escape the hillbilly lifestyle. I had a girlfriend who left her fine home in Southern California because she despised her family's wealth. In the movie My Big, Fat Greek Wedding, we have a girl whose main conflict comes about when she is embarrassed by her ethnic roots.

Crucibles of Condition

An intolerable condition may also be a crucible—such as an illness that two very different characters may join forces to beat. We see this type of crucible used every week as Doctor House tries to solve the latest medical mystery. But you can also set your characters up to fight an economic or political condition—the hunger in India, the tribalism of North Africa.

The condition might be something as mundane as crime in the streets. Policemen who despise one another are often found joining forces to fight drug lords, rapists, and other types of crime.

So as you form your story, consider how you might strengthen your conflicts by developing one or more crucibles.

Reversals

One of the most common plotting tools used in Hollywood is the reversal. You've seen it a thousand times. You're at the high point of a movie, and it appears that the hero is about to make good. Suddenly, the villain shows up and everything goes astray. Your sense of relief turns to dismay. But just as your hero has come to the end of his rope, he suddenly finds a way to pull victory from defeat.

For examples of this, look at the closing scene of *Terminator*, *Alien*, *Jurassic Park*, *Jaws*, or any of hundreds of other movies.

In *The Terminator* our two young lovers escape from Arnold and spend a lovely night together. They're on the open road. They're using cash so no one will be able to track them. All that they need to do now is make it to Mexico and live happily ever after. But somehow Arnold stumbles upon them, and in a great chase scene they blow him to kingdom come. Once again it looks as if they are home free, but now the cyborg—sans flesh and skin—comes stalking toward them from the fire. They flee into a factory and fight the wounded cyborg. In a last-ditch effort at escape, our heroine breaks free, and the poor cyborg gets pummeled to death by heavy equipment.

So when you are plotting your tale, you need to look at your type of conflict, then consider how to deepen that conflict by creating a reversal. For example, if you are writing an "escape" novel about a teenage girl who is desperately trying to flee from her abusive father and escape her home, you will typically come upon a time when she has finally left.

She's made it out the door, down the street, and to the land of milk and honey: Hollywood.

Now, you want to deepen the conflict. To do that, you need to reverse her fortune. That means that you have to put her into greater captivity. Perhaps she'll get picked up by the police, or maybe she'll find herself working for a porn dealer who wants her to star in his next flick, so he nails her into a coffin to soften her up. The major theme is escape, so you need to take away your character's freedom. In some last-ditch effort, perhaps she'll figure out how to escape her demented tormentor by pushing him into the coffin.

On the other hand, if you're writing a story of romance, you would have your character go through a completely different type of reversal. Julia, after much work, finally believes she's going to marry John. But something happens that makes it seem that he is irrevocably lost. Maybe he gets in a train wreck, and the police mistakenly say that he is dead. Maybe another woman is involved. Maybe he's falsely accused of a crime and imprisoned. Whatever the barrier, she must find a surprising way to overcome that barrier to her happiness.

You get the idea. Whatever your major conflict, you simply perform a reversal.

Many writers save the reversal for the highpoint of their story. That's a good idea, but it's predictable. I often find myself intrigued by stories that put a reversal right up in the very first try/fail cycle. It signifies to me that the author is going to work hard on his plot.

Revelations

You've seen the revelation in stories a hundred times. In a romance novel, a rustic hero may finally have a moment near the end of the novel where he tells the girl why his heart is broken, and he can never love again. In an adventure, the hero will almost always have to confront some problem from his distant past. Or perhaps in a fantasy, your hero discusses why he will "never trust a dwarf."

In short, a revelation is a moment where a writer takes time to explain why a character is the way that he is—the cause for his habits or motivations. Revelations may come from the character's own mouth, or might be told from the point of view of a friend or acquaintance, or they might even be deduced by another character.

They can be used for different effects. They can be humorous, endearing, heartbreaking, or horrific.

They work because we sometimes have moments in our own life where we suddenly understand how one single incident vastly affected the life of someone that we know.

My father, for example, was abusive—always hitting and kicking his children. He abused animals, too, and he was likely to shoot the neighbor's dog if it barked too often. (He shot several of the neighbor's dogs over the years.) He worked as a butcher, and on more than one occasion I saw him beat pigs to death by grabbing a snout with one hand, forcing the pig's mouth closed, and then slugging it beneath the eyes. As the pig's snout swelled, it could no longer breathe and it would suffocate.

Yet after he beat you, he'd often weep and beg forgiveness, or else he'd begin to have muscle spasms and in five minutes he'd completely forget what he'd done—blocking it from his mind.

I eventually figured out that he had learned to be violent from my grandfather, a man who had worked as a mobster from the 1920s into the 1960s. When I was a child, my grandfather took a particular fondness to me, and often taught me a sort of criminal catechism in order to prepare me for life. He'd say things like, "Never commit a crime with an accomplice—they'll always rat you out." Or, "The sole purpose of a life of crime should be to maximize your income while minimizing the risk of incarceration." Or, "Some men when they get mad, they yell and scream and cuss and threaten, but they never do anything about their anger. But there's another kind of man, the kind that when he gets angry, he'll come to your house at night with a gun hidden behind his back, and a hole dug in the woods, and when he knocks on your door, he takes care of business without a wasted word of warning, without a threat. I want you to grow up to be that second kind of man."

It wasn't until I was 13 that I learned just how deeply my grandfather's teaching had warped my own father. I asked my grandfather once how many men he had killed. Grandpa fell silent, and my father began naming off a few, using a bragging tone. He said, "Well, the first I remember was those four men whose throats you cut," and he related how my grandfather had brought some men to the house when my father was 12, each of them handcuffed, and had tied them to chairs in the kitchen. My grandfather sent my dad to bed, and all was quiet. In the morning the four men were gone, and my father—weeping from fear and revulsion—was forced to get towels and help mop up the blood from the kitchen floor. "That blood had to be an inch deep," my father said.

"That's the day you became a man," my grandfather told my dad. He explained, "I was working as an FBI agent in those days, patrolling the Canadian border for smugglers. We caught those four fellows, and I wanted their load of whiskey. Of course I couldn't leave any witnesses."

It wasn't until I had heard of that moment that I understood my father. He was violent and twisted, but he'd also spent much of his life running from his own dad, trying to hide evidence of his own past, and trying to fight his own violent impulses. Months later, my father told me, "My dad said that that was the day that I became a man, but that was the day I learned to hate him. That's the day that I decided to leave home." Two months later, at the age of 13, my dad ran away from home. For most of the next 40 years he refused to speak to his father at all.

That's a revelation.

So as you plot your novel, you are bound to create all kinds of interesting characters with various quirks and passions. There may be times when these folks need to reveal how they've become what they are. Consider during the plotting phase if you want to have a moment of revelation.

Twists

When you're writing, it's important to take control of your reader's emotions. You do this by creating sounds, images, or actions. Each time you create an emotional experience, it's called an emotional beat.

One of the best ways to learn to recognize emotional beats is to watch a movie preview. In an action adventure movie, you might see a person say, "You got in here pretty easy, but you ain't gettin' out of here alive." That line is both a humor beat, and a threat. So it can be counted as two beats—humor, adventure. That might be followed by a fight scene—adventure, then by gunshots, adventure—then a glimpse of the hero kissing a girl, who throws him on her bed—romance/lust. Then we might have mysterious music start up, while offstage a voice says, "There's something you need to know"—a mystery beat.

In Hollywood, I studied how to analyze emotional beats in order to gauge just how popular a movie would become, so it can be a great tool for analyzing stories.

When you frequently use the same beats, you create an emotional tone for your story. For example, you can write a novel that starts out with a funny line. A second jest may appear three lines later, a third at the top of the next page. As you do this, the reader begins to anticipate that you're creating a humorous piece, and if your reader happens to be an editor, he may want to purchase your novel for his humor line.

Creating that emotional tone is a must for us as authors, since readers go looking for books based upon the tone. Thus, those who want to read adventure go to the "thriller" section of the bookstore, while those who want wonder might go to the fantasy area.

Of course there are dozens of powerful emotions that you might use to create the overall tone of a work—romance, adventure, wonder, horror, drama, mystery, nostalgia, lust, and so on. Not all of them have a section in the bookstore. Lust literature, for example, has its own special bookstores, while nostalgia literature tends to get lumped into "mainstream."

But if you want to master any genre, you need to learn to arouse the dominant emotion for that genre. In short, if you want to be a horror writer, you need to scare me deeply and often.

However, as a writer, if you continue banging the same note too often, your reader may begin to appear that the work has gone stale. It almost feels as if the author is trying to play a song on the piano with only one note; the song will sound less like music and more like a monkey banging on a piano.

So you as a writer have to change things up. For example, if you watch a good comedy, very often there will come a time when the comedians quiet down, put on a serious face, and say something profound—almost as if that were the purpose of the movie. Do you remember *City Slickers*? There is a great moment where the joking stops and Jack Palance, playing the role of Curly, tells Billie Crystal about his pet theory on the purpose of life, thus defeating the audience expectations.

In another great moment from the screen, in the movie *Jaws*, three men are out on a boat, hunting a shark. As one of them, Brody, throws meat into the water, chumming the shark, the Quint and Hooper exchange boasts, leading to a much-needed moment of humor. The tension for the past thirty minutes has been thick.

But just as the audience begins to laugh, a great white shark lunges up from the water, close enough to bite off a Body's hand, and the audience screams. Steven Spielberg said that he waited for that moment in the theater to see if it would work—turning a laugh into a shriek of terror.

A few nights ago, I re-watched the classic film *The Shining*, starring Jack Nicholson. In one scene, Jack's small son Danny has nearly been strangled, and his wife Wendy rushes in to tell him that in their supposedly empty hotel, a woman got out of a bathtub and tried to strangle the child.

Jack goes to the room where it happened—the much-hyped room 237—to see if there really is a woman there. A beautiful woman gets up naked from the bathtub, and Jack, obviously delighted, goes to kiss her. She falls into his arms, then turns into a rotting old hag. Thus, our emotional beats go from horror, to mystery, to lust, and back to horror.

Whenever we change emotional beats from one thing to an opposite—wonder to horror, romance to drama, humor to wisdom literature—we defeat the audience's expectations. We provide a rest from harping upon the same emotional beat time after time. This actually allows us to make our dominant emotion more powerful in a future scene. It lets the reader get a rest.

So if you're writing a romance, for example, and fear that the romance is going stale, then stop for a moment and consider: what other powerful emotions do I want to draw upon so that I can give my audience a rest? Do I want to put in a quick humorous line or scene? Or is something dramatic called for, or maybe even something horrific?

You may notice that an emotional twist isn't the same as a plot twist. When you twist the plot away from reader expectations, it may or may not arouse strong emotions in the audience. A plot twist demands that the story change direction in some fundamental way. But when you do an emotional twist, very often it occurs on a smaller level, within a single scene.

Whatever you do, look for ways to twist the story in new directions, away from audience expectations. They'll thank you for it in the end, even as you fulfill the promises that you made when you first established the emotional tone for the tale.

Motivation?

In Hollywood, actors will often ask of a character "What's his motivation?" In other words, why is my character a jerk, a fool, a tomboy, an alcoholic, etc. You as an author can't just say, "because." You need to get to the heart of a character.

In particular, "evil characters" are often not properly fleshed out. Why is your dark lord a dark lord? Some people are evil because they are selfish. They're willing to give the whole world pain in order to get a little pleasure. Other people are evil because they were trained to be that way. I remember hating one kid—a bully—as a child, until I heard his father threaten him if he didn't go pick on the fat kid in our class. Other people are evil simply because they're too foolish to see the consequences of their actions. Some people slowly slide into the paths of error over years, while others leap in like a frog into water.

You as an author don't need to show the origins of your characters' traits, good or evil or otherwise, but you should probably know them in the back of your mind just as a way to get to know your character.

Mystery

For any story to work, it has to create suspense—a pleasing sense of anticipation. One way to create that is to create a mystery, a riddle that must be solved, a puzzle that must be put together.

A mystery near the beginning of your story is particularly helpful. Perhaps one of your protagonist's friends dies, and he must search for a killer, or something lost that must be found, or perhaps it is just a philosophical question that the protagonist feels must be answered.

But the mystery need not be dark. It might be something as innocent as a prank that has been pulled, and the protagonist is trying to figure out how to even the score. Or maybe it's a romantic mystery, and your protagonist finds a burning need to figure out the name of the young woman he met at a dance.

The mystery need not deal with people at all. In science fiction novels, a scientist might spend a great deal of time trying to figure out a scientific mystery. For example, in Arthur C. Clarke's award-winning novel *Rendezvous with Rama*, an ancient spaceship is discovered as it swings into our solar system. A scientist is sent to get on the spaceship, but has only a short window of opportunity to study it. Almost the entire novel takes place in the head of one man as he explores this alien spacecraft and ultimately gleans some clues about its creators—and yet never learns all that he yearns to know. There is very little sense of danger in this novel, yet when I was reading it, I couldn't put it down.

In the book *Animals in Translation* by Temple Grandin, the author, a high-functioning autistic who works with animals and studies neuroscience, makes the point that what used to be called the "pleasure center" of the brain is redefined in modern neuroscience as the "searching circuit".

Neuroscientists have found that the searching circuit begins releasing dopamine at the first sign that there's something good to be had (in the case animals it's usually food). i.e.: if a puma sees signs there's a deer on the other side of those bushes, their brain gives them a rush that spurs them to look for it.

The most interesting thing about this is that once the deer is actually seen, the puma's brain immediately stops producing dopamine. The brain is wired to reward searching not finding. The rush comes in the anticipation, not the fulfillment.

Later when the mystery is solved, we get that rush of serotonin that rewards us for solving the mystery.

But the point here is to keep the mystery open, to keep the clues coming, so that we build the anticipation.

Of course for your mystery to be satisfying, you need to create a timetable of clues that your protagonist might find, in part so that you can keep your reader focused on the mystery.

You'll also note that in most murder mysteries, as the detective gets closer to the killer, the detective will normally become a target. In short, the author is intensifying the danger as we near the climax.

So a story that hooks us with a mystery will often turn into a thriller by the end.

Romance

Just as mystery can be a hook in just about any novel, for most novels for teens and adults, one of the strongest hooks is romance. This is especially true for the female demographic—girls ages 12 to 42.

To create a strong romantic angle, all that you really need is to create two people that the audience loves, give them an obstacle to their romance that keeps them apart, and then give them several opportunities to get back together.

Varying Emotions

When you decide to tell a story, you very often commit early to what I call the "controlling emotion" of your tale. You might say, I'm going to write a romance, and thus romance is the primary emotion that you might want to elicit. Or you could say that you want to evoke terror in a slasher book, or wonder in a fantasy, or daring in an adventure.

It might surprise you to know that once you've picked your genre, you've picked your controlling emotion. Orson Scott Card has pointed out that people usually read because there is some emotion that they are lacking in their everyday life. He's right.

To that, I have pointed out that in order to create a sense of story, there must always be an undercurrent of fear.

So when you begin plotting, when you begin considering what your inciting incident is, you don't just say to yourself, "What happens next?" You look at your primary emotions that you want to create, and you'll begin saying, "How can I work toward creating a sense of xxx in my reader?" where the x stands for the controlling emotion.

But a problem often occurs at this point. It's easy to become so involved in brainstorming how to create a certain emotion that you become too focused on that emotion. When that happens, the story begins to sound like a symphony where everyone is just repeating the same note.

So you have to back up at times, not take yourself so seriously, and consider how to vary your emotion.

By knowing what mix of emotions your audience craves, you can design a bestseller. I'm convinced that a sign of J.K. Rowling's genius, for example, is in her unerring sense of what an audience wants. She instinctively recognized that her young audience would crave: wonder, adventure, humor, horror, and romance in the appropriate amounts and in the proper order. She was flawless in evoking the proper emotional beats for her tale.

So when you're writing, keep your mind open. Almost everyone at every age appreciates some humor in their tale. Don't ever write a book without some. Most people will also appreciate a romantic line, regardless of whatever you might want to add. Adventure and horror are also very strong hooks.

I think of a fine story as an emotional symphony. The emotions that I play are the individual notes. My job as an author is to repeat those emotions in patterns that build and play upon each other, and to vary my themes in a pleasing manner.

Introduce Gads

A "gad" is an old Scottish word for a sharp stick used to prod an animal. In a story, a gad is something that one character doesn't like about another. For example, let's say that you have two good friends—cowboys on the range. The protagonist likes to have a varied diet—which includes rattlesnake, woodchuck, and horsemeat. But the sidekick likes to eat beans, lots of beans, and he smells like it. That minor conflict between the two is a gad.

Every character in a story should have something that he doesn't like about the other character. The heroine might wish her cowboy hero wouldn't use puns. He might wish that she would stop talking about old boyfriends.

Very often, you'll find that authors create weak relationships with friends and families just because they don't take into consideration those minor conflicts.

Braid Your Conflicts

Coupled with the concept of introducing gads is the idea of braiding conflicts. As you are plotting, it might help if you consider ways that each major character in your story has a conflict with every other major character. They don't have to be major conflicts, just enough to give a sense that these are real people, with genuine and complex relationships.

Another way to think about it is this: Simply ask yourself questions like, "What is my villain's journey? What was he/she like as a child? What are his hopes, his fears, his loves? How did he sink so low? How much of that journey do I want to show? Do I want to show him making wrong choices when faced with trials?"

Then, once you've got a good sense of your villain, you may look more closely at other characters. For example, let's say that you've got a romantic story line. Many men don't take much time to think about their love interest for a story, but you need to examine her as a character and bring her fully into the story. Where did she come from? Why is she attracted to your protagonist? What's blocking them from getting together? How will she combat it? Why should we love her and care about her?

Once you've answered those questions, consider your protagonist's friends, his "sidekicks." What is their history? Why are they friends? What is the sidekick's personal journey? Does he grow throughout the story?

You should do that with each character. If you have a guide or a contagonist, certainly those are major personalities. Where did your guide come from? What are his successes, his failures? How does your protagonist fit in with his plans?

Even minor characters, such as hecklers can be rounded out this way.

Then, as you write, you look at how each of these characters will interact in their scenes. You weave them together through your story, as if in dance.

Vary Your Conflicts

There are many types of conflicts. Your protagonist should have to face more than one type. For example, let's say that you write a novel about a boy who survives a crash-landing in Alaska. As he struggles to get home, he might face freezing weather, an attack by a bear, an attack by a caribou, and an attack by wolves, all as he tries to find food on a two-hundred mile walk to safety.

The problem here is that he protagonist is facing the same types of conflicts over and over again. These are all external conflicts, man against nature.

What about internal conflicts? The story becomes more interesting if the protagonist has to face his own inner demons. Perhaps he has never been diligent at studying at school, so he doesn't know how to resolve his problems.

Then there are stories about man against man. What if the boy finds an empty cabin and takes a gun to protect himself? But when the cabin-owner gets home, say he's an illegal wolf hunter, the hunter is afraid that the young man will notify the police of his operation. So he goes after the kid, with possible murder on his mind.

Some stories deal with societal conflicts, man versus society. Now let's imagine that the cabin belongs to an Inuit, and he resents the Caucasian boy and his laws. Perhaps he might want to bring his friends in on the hunt, but a young girl in the family decides to try to save the boy. So this could turn into an internal struggle, a clash of societies.

Other stories may deal with religious issues. Perhaps the young man is a devout Catholic, and he becomes angry with

God for putting him into this mess, but later thanks God for the growth that has come through his ordeal.

Look for ways to create interest by using varying the types of conflicts that you create.

Identity Conflicts

The script doctor Michael Hague has said that at the heart of every great character in literature or film, there is a question of identity. He's right.

First, there is the protagonist. What does he see himself to be? Normally he sees himself as an all-right guy, but at some point he will need to confront an inner demon, a hidden weakness. It might be cowardice, laziness, lack of desire to do right, or any other number of things.

Then there may be a "guide" character, usually an older and wiser character who recognizes the protagonist's potential for greatness—and failure.

A romantic interest will also see that potential for greatness, even as her parents and friends deny or ridicule her choice. They may point out that the protagonist is from the wrong side of the tracks, has criminal tendencies, and so on.

A villain may actively try to convert the protagonist to his way of thinking, and seek to destroy his reputation if he doesn't do as told.

Hecklers will of course point out the protagonist's failures, mock his frailties, even as his friends and sidekicks show their faith in him.

Do you see how this works? Any story that doesn't have an identity conflict at its heart will pale in comparison when set aside one that does have such a conflict.

So how does your protagonist see himself? How do others see him or her? In certain types of novels, growth stories and romances, the entire tale often centers on this question.

Center Your Tale

In the opening of a tale, your protagonist may have a number of problems: he may be late for work, and he's lonely. His mother needs him to take her to the doctor, and so on. So we may show him in scenes at work, and with his mother, and perhaps on a date.

But as your protagonist and your antagonist engage in conflict, they're drawn together. The story naturally should begin to focus on them. Thus, if you're writing alternating scenes, the structure of the story reaches a point where we get an almost blow-by-blow description of the epic battle— one from the protagonist's perspective, one from the antagonist's perspective, and so on.

The minor conflicts should all slough away, so that our focus upon the most compelling conflict in the tale is resolved.

Doubling

Writing a novel is like composing a symphony, as I've said—not a symphony of notes, but a symphony of emotion.

I've never read a book on how this might be done, but I'm often very conscious of the emotions that I'm trying to arouse. Robert McKee, in his book *Story*, suggests that we should not compose scenes that strike the same emotional note too often, but he doesn't carry his advice further. I'd like to suggest that there are times when we absolutely must strike the same note more than once in order to give the emotion greater emphasis.

So, here is another plotting tool, a device for heightening an emotion precisely by playing upon it more than once, but by doing so the second time with unexpected intensity. In music it would be like striking the same key on a piano, but hitting the note with great force on the second hit. I haven't heard other writers give it a name, though I'm sure that at least a few others know this technique. I call it "Doubling."

This technique occurs when your viewpoint character anticipates or imagines a certain outcome in a tale and the imagined scene is complete enough so that it alone arouses an emotion.

Here's how it works: imagine that Mary has been craving John. She wants to have his children, and she wants it badly—even from the first page, when she believes him to be an unworthy scoundrel.

So, late in your story, when the audience already cares about John, your heroine daydreams about kissing him. She imagines how fantastic it would be in several long paragraphs. Indeed, she imagines it so well that the imagined scene itself has an emotional impact on the audience.

Then, suddenly, the moment arrives where Mary and John both confess their love and actually do kiss. Here's what you do: you make the depiction different from, better, and more profoundly fulfilling than anything she'd ever imagined.

The concept of doubling simply put is this: you arouse an emotional response by writing in detail about your character's expectations.

This imagined scene arouses the desired response in the reader and sets a bar that you as a writer must jump over. Once you've set the bar, your job is to exceed your reader's expectations brilliantly.

Time and again Dean Koontz uses this technique. In his novel *Intensity*, for example, his protagonist Chyna has a mother who was a moral monster. She dated serial killers and had them murder people for her entertainment. Brutalized from childhood, Chyna spent her life trying to understand what drives serial killers. She's received her master's degree in aberrational psychology.

In the novel, Chyna goes to a friend's house in a remote region where a serial killer is stalking her and her friend's family.

It's gruesome stuff. In one early scene, before Chyna opens a door to the parents' bathroom, she knows what she will find. She imagines that her friend's mother and father will be dead, and she even wonders how it will be done. She imagines it vividly enough so that we the audience are mildly horrified. In fact, he gives us so little that we are forced to imagine it in her stead.

Chyna has heard a murderer and scream in the house, and eventually she makes her way to her friends' parents' master bedroom. After mentioning that she smelled the scent of gunpowder and blood, here's all that Koontz says:

"Chyna had heard no shots. The intruder had evidently had a weapon with a sound suppressor.

"Water continued to cascade into the shower beyond the (bathroom) door. That susurrus splash, though soft and soothing under other circumstances, now abraded her nerves as effectively as the whine of a dentist's drill.

"She was sure that the intruder wasn't in the bathroom. His work here was done. He was busy elsewhere in the house.

"Right this minute she was not as frightened of the man himself as she was of discovering exactly what he had done. But the choice before her was the essence of the entire human agony: not knowing was ultimately worse than knowing."

That depiction sets up a scene. In this case, Koontz cleverly sets up the reader. His last two lines lead you to conjure your own death scene in the bathroom, and he teases you into believing that not knowing is worse than knowing. But in a couple of short paragraphs, he then shows us the murder victim, and with a few brief details exceeds the death scene that you envisioned:

"... she had expected more blood.

"Paul Templeton was propped on the toilet in his blue pajamas. Lengths of wide strapping tape across his lap fixed him to the bowl. More tape encircled both his chest and the toilet tank, holding him upright.

"Through the semitransparent bands of tape, three separate bullet wounds were visible in his chest. There might have been more than three. She didn't care to look for them and had no need to know. He appeared to have died instantly, most likely in his sleep, and to have been dead before he was brought into the bathroom.

"Grief welled in her, black and cold. Survival meant repressing it at all costs, and surviving was the thing that she did best.

"A collar of strapping tape around Paul's neck became a leash that tethered him to a hand-towel rack on the wall behind the toilet. The purpose was to prevent his head from falling forward onto his chest—and to direct his dead gaze toward the shower. His eyelids were taped open, and in his right eye was a starburst hemorrhage."

At this moment, Chyna knows that the murderer taped Paul's eyes open for a reason. She knows that Paul's wife will be dead in the shower. She knows that it will be gruesome, and that the image will stay with her for life. But she also knows that she has to open the shower door. There's a small chance that Mrs. Templeton will be alive, that the killer may have wanted to secure the house and then come back to enjoy her later, save her for desert, so to speak. Chyna has to look.

Well, if you want to know what Chyna finds, you'll have to read the book. Needless to say, once again the writer beats your expectations.

Now, this technique will work for any emotion that you want to hit strongly. To double an emotion, simply create an imagined scene that arouses that emotion, and then show us what happens in such detail that it redoubles the emotional effect.

Haunting

Your character can and should be profoundly moved by events in your book. At times you will need to try to amplify their emotions. One way to do this is by haunting your character, having them recall a moment in time that arouses the desired emotion all over again.

This happens in real life all of the time. For example, if you've had a wonderful date, you might choose to rehearse a conversation in your mind over and over for days, trying to glean every nuance from what a lover said.

Often though, we are faced with situations that genuinely haunt us—that come to our minds unbidden and undesired. This is especially true when we are confronted with acts of violence, such as witnessing a crime or participating in a war, or when we are confronted by death.

A few years ago I had to identify the body of my sister-in-law after she committed suicide. She was a handsome woman, and I had known her for years. But she chose as her method of suicide to ingest a poison that would asphyxiate her. And I cannot think about her without seeing her on her hotel bed, clutching a pearl necklace in one hand while every muscle in her was frozen and contorted so grotesquely that it dramatized with perfect eloquence the human body's need for air. Imagine for a moment that every craving you've ever felt in your life, no matter how profound, was suddenly stamped indelibly upon your face, was etched into your clawed hands, branded into a mouth frozen open far wider than a human mouth should be as if in a permanent scream, and perhaps then you could begin to understand what she looked like.

Sometimes, even four or five years later, at unexpected moments, I would see her there on the tangled gray blanket where she spent her last moments thrashing about.

My sister-in-law was a world-class photographer with displays at dozens of galleries. She used to love to photograph my children, and so I'd often get my flashbacks when I saw my children do something that I wished I could take a picture of, or when I saw one of her photos, or when I saw a woman wearing pearls.

In just that way, your characters should be haunted by memories. Your characters should reflect on powerful experiences time and again so that you gain more emotional momentum from them.

It's not just a matter of arousing emotions, it is in fact a tool for making your characters real. A character whose life feels as if it began when the story started won't feel real to your reader. Your character needs to be created along with a host of friends, family relationships, and powerful experiences that live outside the frame of the story.

So just as doubling allows you to double the emotional impact of a scene (by having a character imagine what will happen, and then writing the scene so that it surpasses the reader's expectations), haunting can let you gain a triple impact from the same incident.

However, you should be aware that you can get more than a triple impact. You can haunt a character almost indefinitely. Often, we write stories about characters who circle a problem. They relive an event, or try to relive or re-imagine it over and over, to see how things could have worked out differently.

As the haunted character finally gains enough distance from the event so that he or she can either learn to cope with it or learn the lesson that the experience teaches, or perhaps begin to understand the nuances of what happened, we begin to see some growth. An example of this is in the movie *Groundhog Day*.

This technique of haunting is your main tool for writing the circling story.

Hence, for certain very powerful key scenes, you may want to consider using all three of these techniques: have your character imagine a scene so that we set the reader's expectations. Then write the scene in such a manner that you exceed those expectations. Then reflect back on that scene at appropriate moments.

Tripling

Just as you can use doubling to hit the same emotional beats twice, you can also add haunting to your doubled scenes to get the most profound effect possible.

For example, near the climax of your romance novel, you might have a scene where your protagonist fantasizes about a date. The protagonist then goes on the date and finds that it is surprisingly romantic, more than she can quite imagine, more than she can really deal with.

At the height of the romantic encounter, you as the writer pull away just as the two slip into the bedroom.

But a third scene, a haunting scene, can be added. Perhaps at work the next day, your heroine is now haunted by what happened in that bedroom—the passion and the wonder of it all.

Using that technique allows you to go for as much emotional impact as possible. Just remember, that the haunting element has to be stronger than anything that the protagonist could have imagined. It must surpass in power even that initial scene where the date began. Creating a scene like this will require you to not only stretch your imagination, it may require you to work long and hard on your treatment, struggling to express the moment in language that is startling and profoundly powerful.

Stacking

Sometimes you need to hit the same emotional note three times, and you don't want to triple your scenes. You may need to "stack" scenes—create a series of similar scenes that drives home a point.

Here's a rather famous example, the story of Scrooge.

Early in *A Christmas Carol*, Scrooge proves his greed in a number of ways. When his nephew asks for a donation for an orphanage in a nearby county, Scrooge asks, "Why? Are there no debtors' prisons?" And at work when his employees are shivering from the cold, he bemoans them a lump of coal in the fire. In the following scene they beg for Christmas day off, and Scrooge demands to know why Christmas should give them all an "excuse to rob me once a year."

So Dickens stacks his scenes in order to prove what kind of character Scrooge is. Later, after his miraculous change, where he confronts three ghosts, we need proof that Scrooge is indeed a changed man. So what does Dickens do? As soon as Scrooge wakens from his long night of dreams, he throws open a window and begs a boy in the street, "What day is it?" He then throws the boy some money to buy a goose to send to the poor—giving the boy extra for the butcher and a nice tip himself. He then rushes into the street in his nightclothes and meets his nephew, promising to get together the next day to find proper homes for the poor (from among his foreclosed properties). He then rushes to the home of his employee, turkey and gifts in hand, and gives the man the day off, and as a last act of compassion, offers to find the finest surgeon to cure Tiny Tim.

Do you see what he is doing? He simply stacks scene after scene to prove that Scrooge is a changed man, with each scene seeking to raise the emotional impact. We suddenly see Scrooge turn from a miser into a man with a mission—to use his wealth to bless the lives of every person he meets.

If you look at classic stories, ones that are told and re-told, you'll find that stacking occurs. For example, take a look at a couple more Christmas classics—*It's a Wonderful Life* and *Miracle on 34th Street*. Then take a look at Mario Puzo's *The Godfather,* where we are introduced to a godfather and shown right from the get-go that he's a powerful man. The technique doesn't just work for feel-good stories.

Growth

I watched the movie *Live Free or Die Hard* for the second time recently. It's a fun action film, and it actually demonstrates some principles we've been discussing. As you watch the ending, you'll see a nice example of a reversal. Bruce Willis racks up a nice body count during the movie, and gets down to two villains left when one of them shoots him. It's a lucky shot, sort of, and therefore unanticipated. After all, a number of talented villains have taken shots at him before. He's eluded everything from bombs to machine guns to sidewinder missiles. So when he gets shot, it takes us back.

But what is interesting is how, once he is in the clutches of this villain, he makes his escape. The antagonist of the film is holding a gun to Willis's chest, but is using him as a shield. Willis looks down at the barrel of the pistol, and gets an idea. He sees the angle of the barrel on the pistol, and then quickly pulls the trigger, making sure as he does that the bullet passes through the fleshy part of his shoulder—missing his lungs, while it then strikes his attacker straight in the chest.

Of course, the scene construction follows the rule in Hollywood which says that a good movie shows you something that you've never seen before. This movie manages this in several places, making it one of those films that you'll look back on ten years from now and go, "Wow, now that was cool film."

But as I was watching it, I felt that there was one thing that it lacked, and it is something that has bothered me in plenty of stories. The villain in the story has no growth cycle. He starts out being a nasty guy, and he maintains a steady level of nastiness. We don't see any hope for redemption, and we don't really see him make any turns for the worse. He's static. Oh, he does get ticked off at Bruce Willis, and he shows plenty of cunning in his attempts to annihilate his foe, but as a villain, he disappointed me.

In a growth cycle, a character typically becomes better than he or she started out. I gave as an example *As Good As it Gets*. In the film, we see Jack Nicholson's character overcome his homophobia, his cruel streak toward dogs, his hatred of women, and a number of other problems. It's the sheer number of growth cycles in him and in all of the other characters that gives the film such charm.

Yet one thing that makes a great villain is that when he starts out, he is not necessarily a villain. In other words, your villain can go through changes and growth cycles, too. As he is confronted by the hero, he may strain and stretch and have an opportunity for growth—but instead fall. In other words, he should end up being a worse person than when he started.

So long as a villain has opportunities for growth, you'll notice that we as an audience will try to suspend judgment. If you watch gangster movies, you'll notice that at times, there really aren't any heroes on a screen. Yet an audience will maintain rooting interest in a villain under a couple of conditions. One of those conditions can be that, he has an opportunity for growth—that he entertains the notion that he will change and do the right thing. Another condition that allows us to gain rooting interest in any person—hero or villain—is that some other character cares deeply for that character. Introduce a mobster with a wife who loves him, and we as an audience will feel more inclined to like him regardless of how despicable he seems. And of course one of the last conditions that will allow us to feel rooting interest in a villain is that he has some redeemable qualities—such as a sense of humor, a charming demeanor, or phenomenally cunning mind.

When you create a villain, don't settle for someone who is generically evil. Give him or her a little duality. Create complex motivations, a full family background, and then plot in an opportunity for growth. It will make them feel a bit more realistic. I used to work as a prison guard. I recall one gang leader who was a notorious killer. One day I was assigned to work out switchboard, where we monitored inmate calls. I listened to this gangster talking to his daughter and to his troubled wife for an hour, and I was amazed at his tenderness with them, and his insights into the human mind. Stone-cold killer—devoted father. It happens all of the time.

It's true that some people really are monsters, but they don't make particularly interesting characters.

Now, here's one trick that might help you remember to create dynamic characters. Many books on characterization will tell you go write up character sheets that list your character's skin color, educational background, medical history and so on ad-infinitum. But I find it far more valuable to always think of my characters in flux. I don't say, "What kind of person is he?" and then try to put tags on him. Instead, I ask, "What is he becoming?"

Duality

Many books on writing will advise you to create "complex" characters. As a new writer I used to muddle around trying to figure out what the author of the writing text meant. Sometimes, the instructor would go on to explain that a complex character was "rounded," that he had a wide list of attributes—a social and religious background, a deep personal history, a well constructed physical presence and habits—all of those things. But once you began writing about that highly developed character, you found that he wasn't quite so complex after all. In fact, no matter how completely you devise a character's emotional and psychological history, that character will not come to life and feel complex unless he has conflicting feelings and philosophies about things. In short, the character has to have "duality."

We see duality in people all of the time. Everyone is conflicted. I mentioned a gang member that I knew in prison who was a stone-cold killer. You'd have thought him a monster based upon his past deeds—until you listened to him council with his distraught wife and his tiny daughter. Suddenly he showed more compassion and wisdom than Oprah Winfrey and Dr. Phil combined.

I remember a woman I used to work with. She would berate and belittle her husband all day long in conversation. But if you ever said anything bad about him—even just to agree with her—she'd tear you up one side and down the other. She loved him desperately and would never leave him, though I often believed she was on the verge of divorce.

Everyone is torn about something. Most of us are torn on dozens of issues.

It is in fact the duality of our characters that makes them feel "complex" or "round."

If you look at Shakespeare's protagonists, they often feel wondrously complex. But if you study them closely, Shakespeare will normally have a major character who is torn up about a central issue. That issue might be honesty, as in *Othello*, or it might be about the nature of love, or honor, or courage. The protagonist often has multiple foils—a lover who pushes him to do one thing, a counselor who begs him to take the opposite tact. Each of these secondary characters will have their own foils—maids of honor, dukes, the court fool, until if you look closely, you will see that the characters almost don't seem to be people at all, only arguments dressed up in various costumes.

Often I have wondered, "Is it really Shakespeare's character that is so complex—or his argument?"

My answer is that it is his argument. Oh, he takes care to dress his characters up in interesting costumes, give them individual personalities and voices, but in his best plays, one recognizes that the ideas and questions presented in the story are more important to Shakespeare than the characters he creates.

A good example of a character who exhibits duality in modern theater is the character of Mal in the defunct *Firefly* television series. (The episodes are well worth watching on DVD if you haven't seen them.) Mal is the captain of a ship not long after the end of a civil war. At times he seems to be cold and pragmatic, a killer even. He has no problem shooting an enemy and leaving him to die—if, by doing so, he can protect his own people, his ship. Yet he also lets his compassion get the better of him. In fact, he is so conflicted that one feels that he is often on a knife's edge. The audience never quite knows what he will do in a dangerous situation. Thus, in the episode "Ariel," when one of his men, Jayne, betrays some of the crew to the Alliance, there is quite a nice moment where Mal opens an airlock and nearly sends Jayne to breathe vacuum. As an audience member, I really believed that he would let Jayne die. It would be the pragmatic thing to do, and we'd seen Mal do the pragmatic thing with enemies often enough.

Now, when you are telling your own stories, you want to try to create that same kind of tension with your characters. You don't want your audience to know what your protagonist will do next. You want to keep your audience off-balance. If your audience does feel that they know what your protagonist is going to do in any situation, it's a sign that your protagonist isn't conflicted enough.

Now, you'll note that I said that your "story" has to have duality to it. I didn't say that just your characters need to have it. You will recall that I mentioned that a setting can have duality to it. We might long to live on Arrakis when reading the latest Dune novel. We might imagine that it would be a heady life, smelling the potent spice, developing super-human mental powers. But then the heat would be intolerable. Hence, Dune is both heavenly and a hell. The same is true in Tolkien's *The Lord of the Rings*. Tolkien's Middle-earth sounds wonderful, so long as you're in the shire, or living among elves. But everywhere else is dark and deadly.

Tolkien even went so far as to create entire races and put them in opposition. The trolls were created by the Dark Lord to combat the ents, the orcs to battle elves, the goblins to fight men, the wargs to compete with horses, and so on. In fact, if you look at it closely, you'll see that each race has its dark enemy—to the point that the world creation feels mechanical and contrived.

So as you are considering your characters and their world, look at how you can increase the tension in your story by adding duality to your world.

The Third Alternative

When most new writers try to write about a character's conflict, they tend to think in absolutes. For example, they might imagine that "John is poor and he wants to be rich, so he decides to rob a bank," or they might decide that "Elaine hates her husband and wants to leave him, hoping to break free from the abusive jerk once and for all."

However, as you begin to write, you'll find that your characters almost always turn out to be more complex than that. In fact, if you consider your character's motivations carefully, the character will become more interesting and believable if you consider "the third alternative."

Let's say that you have a character, Bob, who is poor. He decides that he wants money, and so he is going to rob an armored car.

Bob's conflict seems to be that he wants to move from Point A to Point B.

Poor—to—Rich

Now, let's take some more characters. Imagine that you are writing a very different kind of story. Your story begins with a very young boy named Brett who watches a Miss America pageant and decides that someday, he will win! His basic desire might be shown visually to move from

Homely Male—to—Beautiful Female

A third story: Lisa is a first-year student in college when she meets Kevin, a handsome young professor that she falls in love with. She determines to win him at all cost. Her conflict might be sketched as

Single—to—Married

If you look closely at any of these conflicts—indeed just about any conflict at all—you will find that somewhere between the two points on that continuum there is a place that is true hell.

For example, Bob imagines that by robbing a car he can become happy. Let's say that he works for a bank, so he knows the routine with the armored cars. He knows the drivers. He even knows one who is so detestable that he could rub the sleazeball out and never feel guilty. But think about it: what is it that money really buys? The answer of course might be stated, "freedom from worry." Now, you don't have to have money to gain financial freedom. In our society we imagine that we must live in big houses because everyone else does. We imagine that we need two cars, and three televisions, and five bathrooms, and a pool....

But not everyone buys into that nonsense. A few years ago I picked up an old man in the Oregon desert. He was walking down a long road after making his annual shopping trip. I drove him 90 miles, so we had plenty of time to talk. He lived in a gold mine in the mountains, with only a couple of rattlesnakes for company. He had no bills, no worries, no obligations. He had no job. All he did was scratch around for gold once in awhile. He got by on about $300 per year. To hear him tell it, he was in paradise.

So one way to cope with modern society is of course to reject it—to pack up your belongings and head for the woods. The other way is to beat the system altogether—to throw away all rules of decency and go for broke—to steal that armored car.

Bob of course has been trying to live in the middle. He's been trying to pay his bills with the $8 per hour he makes as a bank clerk, and he finds that his check never stretches far enough. His credit cards are maxed and he's on the verge of bankruptcy. He's discovered that this leads to so much stress in his life, his wife is about to leave him. He finally has come to realize that men with money are sexy, and men without it are nothing. So he thinks that if he scores big, it will solve all of his problems.

But as soon as Bob steals that armored car, he is going to discover that hell is in the middle. Killing the guard isn't going to bring him freedom, it just means that he will always be looking over his shoulder. He's sure from the moment that he pulls the trigger that someday they'll catch him. He finds himself looking in the rearview mirror, straining to hear police sirens. And of course the wife that he hoped to finally please will find out what he has done, and he will lose her.

In short, your job as a writer in plotting your novel is often to look for the third alternative.

Let's go to the story of Brett, the young man who decides that he wants to someday win the title of Miss America. It's an interesting conflict in part because it is so outlandish. Yet if you've ever known a man who has undergone a sex change, you'll find that he has an overwhelming desire to be seen as beautiful and feminine, and there could be no greater validation for that young boy than to someday win the ultimate crown.

But of course, between being male and female, there is something in the middle—a kind of hell. You've probably seen those men who've undergone the operation. If they wait until they're legally old enough to undergo the surgery, their skeletal structure is so affected by testosterone that they never seem quite female—their hands may be too large, their shoulders too broad, their voices too deep. People who get stuck in those failed transgender operations often feel that they are caught in a world whether neither men nor women can accept them. They often find themselves paying for surgery after surgery—

to shave off a bit of nose here, get rid of that bony jaw, enlarge those breasts—and no amount of money spent seems to bring them much closer to reaching their goal.

So as a writer, you would look at that character and write about the third alternative—the hell of living in the middle. And it is hell. Back when I worked in the prison I knew two men who had killed would-be lovers that mocked them for being too masculine.

So now we get to Lisa, the young lady who falls in love with Kevin. She imagines that being married to him would bring her happiness, and perhaps it will. But lots of things happen in a marriage. Kevin might turn out to be a cheat, someone who comes home smelling of other women's perfume. Or perhaps he's from a wealthy family, and Lisa finds that she can never fit in. Or maybe to win him, she has to become a person that she detests. Or what if a week into the marriage, he shows himself to be controlling and abusive? Or what if it turns out that he's not the man that she thought he was—all of his apparent affluence comes from his mob connections?

You get the idea. There may be dozens, or even hundreds of "third alternatives" in the marriage scenario, and it's not until you decide on one that your story will take off.

Now, here is the beauty of using the third alternative technique: when we talked about what a plot is, and how an inciting incident leads a character on a journey to attain some kind of goal, but along the way the protagonist must go through several try/fail cycles? Well, if you sit down and consider your third alternative, you can have your character set off on that quest, and the first try/fail cycle pretty much writes itself.

For example, in Bob's story, he snaps on page one and plans a heist. By page 20 he has a dead guard lying in the seat of his armored car as he makes his getaway, only to realize that even though he has $2.3 million in the back of the truck, he hasn't found the freedom that he'd hope for. Now he's looking in the rear-view mirror, and his ears are straining at the sound of distant police sirens. In fact, in trying to gain financial freedom he has started down a long road to federal prison, and chances are excellent that he will someday look back at his life before the murder and wish to hell that he could go back in time and start over.

With Brett, we can show him realizing from the age of six that he wants to be Miss America. He can start walking like a girl, affecting their movements and batting his eyes, and all it does is creep out his dad and lose him friends. He might realize at the age of ten or 11 that he's turning into a boy, and he must figure out some way to get the process stopped. Maybe he's so driven, that he gets rid of his own manhood in a bathroom, using a kitchen knife. But it isn't enough. He's soon caught in that hell in the middle, trying to figure out how to get his parents to lend him the money to get the hormones necessary to feminize him. Yet even with a set of boobs, he looks in the mirror and everything is all wrong. He finds that he isn't pretty and feminine at all—he's a freak, and even the children on the street see him for what he is.

And of course with Lisa, we can dramatize what she does to land Kevin—the way that she changes her opinions to reflect his, the way that she affects a different kind of upbringing and tries to hide her own family from him until after the wedding. It's not until after the seemingly successful marriage that she begins to find out what kind of a hell she has damned herself to as she learns better who she is, and whom she has married.

So as you plot your story, consider your character's motivations well, and consider how the third alternative might help you generate the opening to a story while at the same time giving it greater depth.

The Rule of Threes

You'll notice the number three appearing everywhere in writing. It has to do with the way we learn.

Budrys points out that "That which you tell your audience three times, they will believe." So, for example, when describing a storm, you need to describe it three times. You might describe the sound of the wind howling outside and rain splattering on a window (aural description). You might then follow it with a physical description, the feel of rain spattering your protagonist's face as he opens the door, the taste of the storm on his tongue. You then follow it by him seeing the sheets of rain falling by the porch light, just as a tongue of forked lightning strikes out on the hill. Do you see what I've done? I created an image using three senses, but describing the storm each time.

In the same way, in attempting to resolve a problem, a character must make three attempts. This is called the Rule of Three, and the reason you must have three attempts is obvious, if you think about it.

Imagine that you are going to the subway, and while on the platform, a man bumps into you hard enough so that you wonder if he's trying to push you onto the tracks.

He apologizes to you profusely, explaining that he stumbled. You file it in your mind as a fluke—an accident, a one-time happening.

Now, imagine that tomorrow you are waiting for the subway, and the same man stumbles into a woman, nearly pushing her onto the tracks.

Is it a fluke? You don't think so.

You accost him, and he apologizes more profusely; he grovels even. He explains that, yes, he did bump you yesterday, and he bumped the woman this morning, but it was a mere *coincidence*. He's been working 20-hour days, and he has muscle control problem—that's why he can't drive, and has to take the subway.

What do you do? Do you let him off the hook, or do you trash him? You let him off the hook, unless you're a cynic. After all, we've all had bad days.

But you're much more suspicious, so suspicious that you can't sleep well that night. So the next day, you hide in the subway, in the shadows, and you watch for the man. Sure enough, he enters the subway and looks around furtively.

Or is it furtively? Are you just imagining it?

He steps toward the platform as a train comes hurtling through the tunnel. He stumbles, and knocks a child in front of the train!

Among the screeching breaks and the wail of the child's mother, you hear the horrifying death shriek.

Was it a fluke? Was it a coincidence?

No, it was a pattern!

And heroes must break patterns.

If you have a sense of justice, you will of course go out and make sure that this fellow is prosecuted.

Indeed, if you've also got a good sense of timing, you might even manage to break the pattern once you recognize the villain's intent.

But as Budrys points out: if the hero does not have to make three attempts to resolve a problem, then the problem was not difficult enough in the first place. And any villain who does not at least try to victimize people more than twice isn't really a quite villain—yet.

The Hourglass of Evil

In many tales, in the beginning evil is seen to be "distant" from the protagonists. The orcs are rampaging in far lands in *The Lord of the Rings*, while in *The Christmas Carol*, Scrooge is asked to donate money to orphans in a distant county.

But as the tale progresses, the evil draws closer to the protagonist. Black Riders enter the Shire, poverty strikes in the homes of Scrooges' employees.

Eventually, at the end of the tale, evil is seen in the hearts of the protagonists. Frodo discovers that he cannot give up the ring at the Crack of Doom, while Scrooge learns that his own selfishness lies at the heart of the troubles around him.

Thus, there must come a turning point where your character sees the evil in himself and resolves to either change, or is destroyed. It is only when evil is subdued in the hero's heart, that changes can be made abroad, and good can sweep over the earth.

Because of this, as you plot, you need to consider carefully how to work toward the turning points for each of your characters—whether they seize the opportunity to change or not.

Spectacle

Some sights are so riveting, so compelling, that you cannot take your eyes off of them. Remember when the twin towers collapsed? The eyes of the entire nation were on it.

Similarly, as you write a book or screenplay, there may be moments when a spectacle appears, to you, an image that you just feel that you have to capture perfectly.

When that happens, take time to stop and create that image fully. You may write it out of context completely—as a set piece that you will insert into the story when you come to the proper location.

Add a Thematic Line

As you begin to plot, you may discover that your story has a theme that you wish to elaborate on. For example, I realized in a recent novel that I was dealing with a theme of "becoming one in heart." So I had to stop and wonder, how well does my current story handle that theme? Do I need to add more scenes, or perhaps embellish a dialog here and there?

Look for scenes that might be interspersed throughout the story where you may elaborate upon the theme. Consider how the theme might interlace with the action so that the story changes or grows in new directions.

Put Your World in Jeopardy

It isn't just characters that can change or grow or face jeopardy during the course of a story. Sometimes the world can change in alarming ways, or in beautiful ways.

In Tolkien's *Lord of the Rings,* the jeopardy broadens. Frodo goes on his journey to save the Shire, but discovers that the danger threatens Rivendell, Lothlorien, and distant lands beyond his imagination. In short, the whole world is in danger.

Similarly, in a good thriller, we may start off with a tiny army clerk who finds herself targeted by an assassin, but as the story grows we learn that others are also slaughtered, and that an entire nation will crumble if an evil plot isn't thwarted.

Is this kind of change a possibility in your story? If so, you need to decide how to dramatize your changing milieu.

Create an Epic

An "epic" story is one that creates a sense that the reader has experienced much of the world, or caught a snapshot of life. An epic feel in a story can be created a number of ways.

—You may create an epic feel by having a wide variety of characters from different classes—the upper classes, working classes, and so on. These may span women and men, old and young. In short, we get to see the world from the viewpoints of dozens of people, and hearing them speak in their own unique voices.

—You can create an epic feel by following characters over the course of a lifetime. For example, you might start a tale with a young man and woman who fall in love as children, grow into adults, marry, become parents and grandparents, and then add in the story lines of some of their offspring, creating a multi-generational saga.

—You can create an epic feel by visiting different parts of your world, different climes, so that you set parts of your story upon the water, other parts in mountains, etc., so that the story seems to span the world.

—You can create an epic feel by making sure that your tale spans the seasons of the year as well as the seasons of life.

SECTION 3

THE PLOTTING PROCESS

PROMISING STARTS TO A NOVEL

We've been talking about brainstorming your novel and outlining it. I've also talked about how as a writer I often sit down before composing and set certain goals for myself on what I'd like to accomplish as I write. Given this, I've determined that there are several things that I want to do in my opening chapters.

When I talk about writing an opening, what I'm really talking about is the portion of a novel that typically occurs before my protagonist discovers that he has a "major, life-altering problem on his hands." This might actually be more than a chapter. It might be four chapters, or five. In Hollywood there is a rule of thumb that says that your opening is usually about 1/10th of a movie. That rule of thumb often turns out to be remarkably accurate. It's almost as if we have some internal clock that drives us, telling us how much time we should take at the start of a book.

Of course if you look at a book or movie, you'll find that this portion of a story is often easy to delineate. I'd say, for example, that in *The Wizard of Oz*, our "first chapter" is the part of the story that occurs just before Dorothy's house falls on the witch. In *Star Wars Episode IV*, the opening chapter would include everything up to the point where Luke Skywalker realizes that he will have to go help save Princess Leia. In my own novel *The Runelords*, the opening includes everything up to the point where Gaborn Val Orden discovers that the kingdom of Heredon is about to come under attack. In *The Lord of the Rings*, the opening is probably everything that happens up to the time when Frodo discovers that he will have to leave the shire.

So if we look at a book that is 500 pages long, we might say that the opening of the novel is the first 50 pages.

Now, I'm not going to tell you what to write or how to start your book. As you consider possible scenes, you will find your own way of doing it. You might want to start your novel at rest—your heroine at home in the evening doing her wash, talking to a neighbor over the fence as she hangs out her clothes. You might want to go in with some significant conflict—perhaps the president of the United States calling Boris Yeltsin and offering to "duke it out" in a nuclear war. Maybe you'll want to let us know the nature of your major conflict first, and so you'll write a prologue where a deranged killer snatches a child off the streets of Anytown, USA.

But if you look closely at openings, I've discovered over the years that no matter how you start, there are some things that you should consider.

Sol Stein, a famous editor, once made an informal study with several other editors who lurked in bookstores in New York, watching potential customers pick up books.

Customers, as you know, will typically be interested in a book based on the cover and title.

They might flip to the back of a book to see what kinds of blurbs other authors or critics might have given the book—but probably not. The cover and title are what they focus on. In fact, once I was selling a children's book called *Rindin the Puffer* at some Christmas festivals. I'm very proud of the cover quotes on our book, but I found that of over 500 sales, only two consumers bothered to read them!

After glancing at the cover, the readers then open the book and read a bit. Stein says that his editors found that in every single case, the customer made a choice to buy the book that they browsed through based upon the first three pages. In fact, he found that some 90 percent of the buyers read only the *first* page.

So, as an author it's important for you to make a good impression right at the start. Here is my first piece of advice: Every story should start with promises made—promises that you must keep.

It may be that you're writing a story about a fascinating person, in which case your opening should tease us with a scene or narrative about that person. "John loved women with pale throats—when he saw one, he could not help but follow her home, and then stare into her window night after night."

It may be that you're writing a story that deals with a fantastic setting. In which case you might open with that setting. "John gazed down over the Opal Valley at Ralta, where the sun shimmered on the mists rising from the thermal pools, creating a dazzling opalescent light show above turquoise pools and ground streaked salt-white and the saffron color of sulfur."

If you are showcasing your talents as an author, then perhaps a display of your talent is called for. William Gibson, in his novel *Neuromancer* opened with a line something like, "The color of the sky was the dirty blue of a television set tuned to a dead channel." The metaphor was wonderful, for it demonstrated that his viewpoint characters were so distanced from nature that they had to turn to metaphors from technology in order to describe it.

If you are more interested in telling a story, you might tease the audience by promising a story. Here are a couple of my opening sentences. "Tana Rosen met Karl William Ungritch three times in her life—twice before the end of the world and once long after." Or "Kaitlyn promised to love me forever, and whether that was ten thousand years ago, or a hundred thousand, or more, I didn't know."

In both of those openings, I promise to tell a story.

So, I suggest that the opening to your story show promise to a reader. Look objectively at your story and consider which elements most fascinate you about it, and which are most likely to draw the reader. Then devise an opening that highlights those facets to your story. And you don't have to show just one promise—you can make dozens of promises You can hint at thrilling conflicts, show two or three fascinating characters, give us an interesting sentence, and write it all beautifully—in a single page!

But remember, your opening page or three is an advertisement for your book. If you make promises, you must keep them. If you hook your readers with fascinating characters, and then become lazy and have those characters fall into stereotypes by page 25, your readers will notice. They might not consciously recognize what is wrong, but at some level they will discover that this book isn't exactly what they'd hoped for, and they'll put it down. I can't tell you how many times that happened to me back when I worked as the first reader for the Writers of the Future Contest.

Only make promises that you can to keep. If your opening page promises a five-star book, but you only deliver a three-star book, your fans and critics alike will feel cheated, and instead of praising your strengths, will merely cry "Fake!"

Now, as most of you know, many a writing instructor will talk about how you should create "hooks" for your reader. A hook is a metaphor. Just as a fisherman hooks his fish and drags it into land, a writer supposedly does the same with his reader. A "strong hook" is a line or two that will supposedly thrill a reader into pressing forward.

It's not an apt metaphor. The promises a writer makes to his reader are often subtle and many, and every sentence that you pile onto your tale should have barbs that bite into your readers' consciousness. In short, you can't rely upon a good line or two to hook your reader into a book. You should have dozens of hooks. But here are the things that your opening lines, paragraph, and chapters should typically do:

—Introduce a conflict, character, and setting—all while setting your hooks.

—Establish resonance with the reader.

—Create rooting interest in your protagonists.

—Promise the reader a powerful experience if he or she reads on.

—Induce stress in the reader.

—Advance the plot.

Introducing Your Conflict, Character, and Setting

When you start to write a story, it seems self-evident that you must answer some basic questions: "Who is doing what?" "Where and when are they doing it?" "What's happening?"

Yet you would be surprised at just how many authors fail to accomplish this. There are a number of ways to goof up. One of the most common problems is that the author has two characters who are talking to each other, and as they talk, the author decides, "You know, this story could be happening anywhere in the world. It could even be happening any when. I guess that I don't really need to tell the reader where and when it is happening."

And if you make that argument, in some modern writing courses your teacher might applaud you. But any editor in New York will recognize that you're a rank amateur. In part, the story will fail because the reader will have a lingering doubt in the back of his mind. But more importantly, one of the largest draws for readers is the element of transport. The reader wants to be taken away from this mundane world and travel to a new one.

As an author, your job isn't just to tell the reader where and when the story occurs, it is to create the story. That means that from moment to moment you must control what your reader hears, sees, smells, tastes, feels, and even thinks. You must control not just the physical sensations of your reader, but also the reader's thoughts and emotions.

In other words, "transporting" your reader doesn't just consist of moving him or her to another place in their imagination. In order to fully transport a reader, you must work at taking control of both his or her thoughts and emotions. Once you do that, your reader will become fully engrossed in your work, and hours later will look up from the book wondering just how long they were under. That is your ideal.

A good example of this was in the papers about 20 years ago. A fellow was in an airport reading a novel by L. Ron Hubbard called *The Buckskin Brigade*. He became so engrossed in the novel that when the flight attendants announced that it was time to board, he missed all half a dozen announcements. The plane had been gone for an hour before he realized what had happened, so he boarded the next flight home. When he arrived home and opened the door, all of his family had gathered, and everyone was in tears. "What's wrong?" he asked, fearing the worst. In shock, his family said, "Your plane went down. Everyone was killed."

Of course, as a result of this, Hubbard made the news on every major television network, and sales of the book soared. So that's your goal as a writer, to engross your reader, to bring the story to life right out the gate.

Now, usually when a new writer messes up, they neglect to tell us about the setting. But I see other problems. One other common glitch that you come across with new writers is this:

> *The wizard stood above the cauldron, inhaling the bitter scent of his potion as it boiled. Long white brows poked out beyond the brim of a battered robe. The man was old and haggard, his eyes reddened from too many days on too little sleep. Long had the hunter been seeking the ingredients for this potion, and so his robes were brown and stained. He looked over to where his brother lay in a twisted heap, weakened by the winter fever. Jessot's hand grasped a tong, thrust it into the green gurgling brew, and began to stir.*

So my question for you, astute reader, is how many people are in the above scene? Do you think that I'm talking about one, or could it be five? Are the wizard, the man, the hunter, and Jessot all the same person?

The problem of course is that the writer wants to create an image in our minds but feels that if he gives us a name—without any hint of the gender of the character, a basic description, or the character's age. So the writer tries to work up to giving us the name.

In this case, in my mind I'm describing one person, and I signal that by lumping the information into one paragraph. But not all writers would do that. I recall once trying to read a story where I sat down with a piece of paper, and in the first three pages found 16 distinct people on the bridge of a star ship. I was several pages in when I suddenly realized six of the people described were in fact only one person—the captain. It turned out that a second character, described variously as a dangerous dark-haired assassin, the science officer, and his wife—was a second person on the ship. I actually had to phone this person and ask how many people were on that deck. Turned out there were only four.

In short, when you introduce a new character, give that character a name and don't be afraid to repeat it. Once we have a name, you can spend your time describing that person in detail.

So with any tale, you should let us know who the characters are, where they are, and you should name some problem that they are facing. I used to have a rule when I was editing. If I didn't know what was going on to some degree within 300 words, I rejected the story.

You don't have to open the tale with, "Roland Gale lost his left foot, and therefore the love of his life, at 3:08 p.m. on October 1, 1997,"—but that would be a perfectly acceptable start, and far better an opening than a weather report.

As for the conflict, here is a trick that you can use. You don't have to introduce the major conflict of your novel on the first page (though a fine example of introducing the major conflict on page one can be seen in Brandon Sanderson's *Elantris*, and also in Anne Rice's *Interview with a Vampire*).

You can in fact start a tale by introducing one conflict, a minor one that is easily dispensed with, and then moving to another, and another, and another—until you reach your major conflict. By doing this you can have conflicts, but the major conflict might not be revealed for hundreds of pages into the novel. Consider, if you will, Hitchcock's classic thriller *Psycho*. (I'll let you study the opening to see how it was done.)

For example, let's say that you're writing a fantasy. You may have your character impatiently waiting for a coach outside an inn (conflict 1) when he hears a cry down a nearby alley (conflict 2) and timidly moves into the shadows in an effort to see what is going on without getting caught (conflict 3), then he discovers that his uncle has been stabbed and is being robbed (conflict 4).He draws his sword knowing full well that he hasn't the skill to use it against even one determined opponent, much less three (conflict 5) but he hopes to create a ruse (conflict 6) and so shouts as if to unseen friends, "Rupert, Jean, he's over here! Help!" He then lunges at the attackers (conflict 7). By paragraph three he might be fighting for his life (conflict 8), and worrying about what his lover Constance will think if he should die (conflict 9). He hears shouting out on the street and imagines that the robbers have a lookout who has come to their aid (conflict 10), only to see that their lord has come—a ghoulish skeletal mage (conflict 11)—and you know what folks, we're only into this tale four paragraphs and haven't even started getting close to the good part!

I call this technique "stacking your conflicts," creating a web of conflicts early and consistently so that the reader becomes deeply hooked long before he or she knows what the novel is really about.

Now, I mention here that in your opening chapter you'll need to do this. But you should also know that in every chapter where you change a setting or character, you'll have to do the same thing, You'll have to introduce your new characters, setting, and conflicts for the chapter. So each time that you open a chapter in a novel, make sure that you've got all three of these major elements covered.

I mentioned that I had a rule of thumb as an editor: If you don't introduce a major character, setting, and conflict within the first 300 words of a short story, your story was rejected. I once spoke to Algis Budrys about this, and he wasn't anywhere near as lenient as I was. With him you got 150 words.

But I should note that I had a reason for allotting more space. You see, there are different standards in storytelling around the world. If you read *Aurealis*, a science fiction magazine in Australia, or you read *Interzone* in England, you'll note that our friends across the seas often give themselves more time to start a story. They write at a much more relaxed pace, and I myself often love the depth and power of their ideas (over there, big ideas in short fiction are a staple, unlike here in the US, where I sometimes feel that authors have quit trying). Given that I was judging a global contest instead of a US magazine, I made allowances.

I've already touched on a few problems that I saw too frequently in openings, problems that dealt with a lack of characterization, lack of setting, or lack of conflict. Here are some more.

Only one character is introduced. Far too often I would read a story where, "Nathan sat on a rock overlooking the valley below as he watched the sunrise. This is the last sunrise I'll ever see, he told himself...." The writer will usually then proceed to give a weather report. I saw this a lot, with perhaps 30 percent of all stories.

Now, maybe you see the problem, and maybe you don't. The problem is that stories revolve around conflict, and when you open with only one character, you're not putting that character into direct conflict. You might narrate a problem that he or she has had recently, or you might then move into a flashback, but both techniques are far weaker than introducing us to multiple characters in the opening scene.

It's far better to open with an argument or with characters actively working to resolve a problem or with multiple characters discovering that they've got a huge problem than it is to open with a static scene where someone is just thinking.

Another weakness that deals with characterization has to do with characters who don't act. A character that doesn't recognize a problem, doesn't want to talk about a problem, or doesn't want to deal with a problem can be real trouble.

Interestingly, many new authors tend to want to write about people who want to just talk about their problems, and the author feels that "discussing some different options" is the same as trying to resolve the conflict. But it doesn't work that way. Sadly, I've read stories where the writer decides that the characters would rather just live with their problems than try to resolve them.

I didn't talk about mistakes that I frequently saw in writing about conflicts, but there are some.

The first one of course is that no conflict is introduced early in the story. Perhaps the author gets far too involved in describing the weather (note that I'm harping on weather forecasters?), or the writer spends a great deal of time describing the scenery. Did you ever have a writing assignment in college where you were supposed to describe a brick wall for five pages? Sometimes those exercises get sent to contest judges as stories.

Now, don't take this as a blanket criticism of stories that start with description. If you're the type of writer who writes breathtaking description and this is a primary draw in your writing, then doing so in a perfectly viable option for you. I've read mainstream writers whose use of language is the primary attraction in a story. Love 'em. But in most genre fiction, it just doesn't work.

Another common problem is that the author wants to open the story with a scene that shows us "life at rest." He wants to show us what life is like on a good day, a normal day, before all hell breaks loose. That's a reasonable approach to storytelling. The mistake in this case happens only when you don't get to something interesting soon enough.

Perhaps you want to emphasize how much a husband loves his wife, or a mother loves her daughter—just before you take that wife or daughter away. So you try to create a loving, touching scene.

Your instincts might be right.

But I've read 15-page conversations between husbands and wives at the openings of stories, conversations where the only point was to let you know that these two folks love each other, and that little bit of information just doesn't pull the story's weight. Far too often, these openings are syrupy sweet, and the reader just feels manipulated. So I'm not going to say that it should never be done; you just need to do it cleverly.

A third mistake is what I will call "the mystery problem." Usually the story opens with a man or woman running for their lives—from what, the readers don't know. The writer won't tell us. This opening is seen so often that most editors in America will reject it out of hand. It's cliché.

The mistake mentioned above is actually just one form of a more common problem with new writers, a problem that I call "false suspense." Real suspense arises when a character has to face a problem—one that requires all of his or her toughness and wits to resolve—and the audience has to genuinely worry that the hero will fail.

But writers sometimes try to create false suspense. They might write a scene, for example, where a woman is walking through a deserted, poorly lit parking lot in a dense fog, trying to find her car. She hears footsteps coming toward her, and remembers reading about a serial killer in the papers. In terror she fumbles for her keys and races to her car. Just as she gets to it: a dark stranger steps out and says, "Hey, sweetheart, need help with those keys?" Of course the mysterious stranger turns out to be her husband, and she knew that he was coming to the car all along. You've seen this trick used in crummy horror movies a hundred times. You felt cheated when you paid for it, so don't try it with real editors.

Closely related to false suspense is "false mystery." I've seen writers try to hide the names of characters, the sex of character, the basic problems that the character is trying to deal with, or how an attempted resolution ends. The author might have a fight scene, and then not let the reader know who won—that type of thing. The idea, it seems, is that if you have a little mystery in a story, it will lure the reader into keeping up. But a mystery needs to be real, it needs to be fascinating. If an author is just refusing to tell you the basic information that you need to understand the story—the character's name—he's cheating.

So those are a few more problems to avoid when you start a story.

Creating Rooting Interest Early in Your Novel

In opening your novel, I've become more and more convinced over the years that one of the most important things you can do is to begin creating rooting interest in your protagonist(s). The reason for this is simple: the more powerfully sympathetic that a character becomes to a reader, the more eager the reader will be to find out what happens to that character—and the more powerful the climax of your story will be. In short, creating a magnificently powerful tale begins by creating sympathy for and rooting interest in your primary characters.

Now, how do you create characters that your readers will care about?

In part, you do it by creating characters who mirror your readers. A few weeks ago I mentioned that the most powerful draw for a movie is that it has a character who is roughly the same age and sex as the viewer. It's a subliminal draw, but it is the single most powerful draw.

This means that when you write a story, you will of course be populating it with at least one character who will appeal to your primary market. If you're writing for teenage boys, then your protagonist will be a teenage boy. You might think that you can get away with having a protagonist who is of the wrong age or sex, but you're wrong. Teenage boys want to read about teenage boys—not about teenage girls, not about geriatrics. Unfortunately a lot of writers don't seem to get this. In the way of children, a teenager can probably develop some rooting interest in an older character—up to the late 20s. But once that character begins looking more like the boy's dad than the boy, forget it.

So your characters need to be roughly the same age and sex as your target audience.

Next, your character's internal landscape must roughly match your reader's internal landscape. Your characters' hopes need to be your readers' hopes. This means that if you imagine your reader to be noble and idealistic, then your character should probably be so, too. This is tremendously important. Let's say that you have a reader, a woman who is 19. What kind of person are you when you're 19?

When my daughter was that age, she ran a kiosk in a mall. The day before Christmas, one of her employees, a girl of 17, got thrown out of her house by her parents. My daughter felt very sorry for her, and loaned her friend the car, so she could go home and talk to her parents. Well, you can probably guess what happened next—the girl kept the car for over a week (claiming that it had broken down and was in the shop). She slept in it with her boyfriend and a couple of other strangers and the friends were heavy smokers, so they ruined the interior. They ran the car into a snow bank and wrecked it. The girl and her friends then got into the car's glove compartment and found an electronic key to her hotel. They tried to break into her hotel room, but the key only got them through the security doors in the lobby—so they got behind the manager's desk, made a key to an empty room, and partied it up in that. The police caught the girl and arrested her several times in the course of the week—for stealing my daughter's car, for stealing a room, and for shoplifting at the mall where she worked.

Now, as a parent over 50, I have to tell you, I'm a bit cynical. If a kid gets thrown out of her house by her parents on Christmas Eve, I figure they've got a danged good reason. I wouldn't loan the girl my car. I wouldn't give her a nickel. I wouldn't spare her any sympathy.

But do you know what? At the age of 19 I probably would have done just what my daughter did. In short, I was naive and idealistic, and at one level at least I'm proud of my daughter's innate decency.

But have you read John Grisham? He's writing for men my age, and in his stories, his characters are a bit more cynical. He understands that our elected officials are pretty much all on the take. He writes about how lawyers tend to run con jobs. He lays bare methods used to launder money or rig elections. He talks about how companies like Enron get into trouble.

Now, I get that. His internal landscape is just like mine. After all, I used to be a prison guard. My grandfather worked for the mob and took me under his wing when I was a child, teaching me how to run whore houses, run smuggling operations, and how to rub out in the competition. More than that, I worked in Hollywood for awhile—and I became acquainted with sleaze at levels that my grandfather never dreamed of.

In short, I love reading Grisham because he's just as cynical as I am. The inner landscape of the writer in this case—and usually the characters—nicely matches my own.

So give your readers someone that they can relate to, and that will go a long way toward creating rooting interest.

But there's more. There are some almost universal traits that you might consider. Give your characters the desire for acceptance or love, the desire to overcome their own weaknesses, a hope for mankind, a love of honor and decency—in short, give them our most common virtues, and you will create rooting interest.

You don't have to express those attributes in positive terms. You can express them as negatives. Instead of a hope for life, you can give them a fear of death. Instead of hope for love, you can give them a fear of loneliness. Instead of hope for approval, you might give them a fear of dishonor, of rejection by family and friend.

So all of our most common fears can also be used to create rooting interest for your character.

Many writers in mainstream say that we must give our characters weaknesses in order to make them "more realistic." In short, one popular author suggested that if you have a teenage protagonist, you should give him a masturbation problem and a drug habit, make him despised by friends because of his acne, make him lonely, morose, and lazy. After all, this author will tell you, that's how teenagers really are, aren't they?

There are some problems with this. First of all, the writer's job is not to depict reality. That's not what writing is about. "Realism for realism's sake" is as foolish a notion as is "Art for art's sake." We do not read in order to confront reality, we read because we want to fill needs that reality isn't satisfying.

His argument is fundamentally wrongheaded.

Let me say this as clearly as possible: You should recognize that each time you associate some vileness with your protagonist, you create a barrier between that protagonist and your reader. Your reader may very well not have an acne problem. Some kids never even think of masturbating, and they'd be horrified to learn that others do. I don't think that many people are really lazy. A normal, healthy person naturally works. (Lazy people are usually suffering from a physical ailment—low thyroxin levels, disorders of metabolism, such as diabetes, or from depression.)

If you go too far, you can easily create a protagonist that will eject your reader from the story. You might decide, for example, to create a protagonist who is a racist. Now, I know that there are racists in the world, but I've got to tell you, I don't care if your Nazi wants love. I don't care if he wants respect, a decent job, or to break his drug habit.

In short, take care that you don't make your characters too vile. If you do give your protagonists weaknesses, a couple of them are sufficient; and if the protagonist recognizes those weaknesses and sees them as something to overcome, then your reader will be much more likely to sympathize with him.

You can get away with a lot, if your protagonist hates himself for his weaknesses. Look at the movie *Jerry McGuire*. In it, Tom Cruise has one moment where in a drunken haze he gropes his co-star. He was really a creep, and as I saw that scene, I thought, "Man, this movie is over for me." But then Cruise did something cool—he begged for forgiveness, and he did it so convincingly that, for me, at least, it worked. Sometimes the technique can be more subtle. Have you seen the James Bond movie, *Casino Royale*? In it, we have a James Bond who is a sociopath. He's admirable in ways—inhumanly driven, quick thinking. But he has a problem—he seems to be incapable of love. So the entire movie revolves around him learning to love a woman—and then losing her. Though the performance is subtle, we as audience members tend to recognize what is going on.

So when you create your character, I'd suggest that you consider ways to make that character someone that we want to spend time with.

We tend to care more about characters who care deeply about something, who are committed to something. Perhaps they care about their families, or have a powerful love for their country. Maybe that character loves his horse, or is uncommonly honest or honorable.

But you can consider other ways to make characters likable. We tend, quite frankly, to be drawn to people who are attractive. In writing, I don't think it matters much whether your character is physically attractive. As writers we lay our characters' hearts bare. It's their hearts that the reader must admire.

Think about the attributes you admire in others. If you're a woman, do you like men with power? The truth is that power and wealth tend to be very attractive to most women. But if you look at polls, a good sense of humor is what most women will say they want in a man.

As a reader, I have to admit that I'm also drawn to characters that are eccentric. By that, I don't mean that the characters are odd-looking. I'm not going to respond positively to your character just because he has a hunchback and a peg leg. I mean that I tend to look for characters that I find intriguing—characters who have interesting ways of looking at or reacting to the world, characters with sharp minds and keen insights. I tend to like characters who don't much give a damn about what the rest of the world thinks about them.

But that's just me. You probably have your own quirks, and because of that, you'll develop your own audience.

In short, as you begin your own tale, look early for ways to begin developing rooting interest in your character. I think that in a novel, if you have a scene or two dedicated primarily to simply exposing what kind of person your protagonist is, those are scenes that as a reader, I would value.

The Most Important Thing at the Start of Your Novel

I pointed out a good opening should "Promise the reader a powerful emotional impact if he or she reads on."

I'm convinced that people read stories primarily for emotional impact. If we wanted information, we'd be reading news magazines. If we wanted beautiful language, we'd go for poetry. If we wanted insight, we might be reading philosophical texts.

But when we read a story, we go to it looking for a number of things. We might hope to be surprised by the twists that take place in a murder mystery. We might read a romance looking to fall in love with a protagonist. We might pick up a science fiction novel hoping to be swept off to a wondrous new world—and so on.

So when a reader picks up a story, he or she begins looking almost instantly to see if these kinds of emotional needs are going to be met.

In fact, have you ever noticed that we don't really have genres? We tend to buy our books based upon the emotions that they promise to arouse—romance, thrills, horror, wonder (in science fiction and fantasy), justice in westerns, and so on.

All readers, before they ever crack open a book, begin looking at stories hoping for clues as to what the big emotional payoff will be.

Now, I can think of a number of ways to promise a powerful emotional experience.

Yet authors often fail to recognize what their readers' needs are. I can't tell you how many times I've read stories for science fiction or fantasy contests that failed to arouse any sense of wonder at all – tens of thousands, obviously. In the same way, I've seen horror stories that fail to arouse a chill, and dramas that were just plain dull, and comedies that were more grotesque than clever.

So how do you convince a reader to continue on?

Sometimes an author's sure use of prose is enough to convince me to read on. If you write skillfully, if your descriptions are crisp and your characterization is sure-handed, I'll probably read on just because I know that I'm in the hands of a pro.

In yet other cases the use of a great opening hook will do it, or perhaps the author's subtle use of foreshadowing.

Just as often, a compelling storyline will do the trick. If you open with a compelling problem that confronts your characters, that will carry your reader a long way into your tale.

But the single most effective way to promise a powerful experience is to write an opening that in itself creates an emotional impact.

The first scene can be anything—a funny incident that introduces one of your protagonists, or perhaps an argument that leaves your reader shocked. Maybe you'll write a scene that will leave your reader admiring your protagonist and cheering for her, or perhaps you'll introduce your tale with a gruesome murder that will leave the reader horrified but burning with intrigue.

In short, whatever you do in the opening of your story, a great opening scene will almost always find some way to arouse a powerful emotional response in the reader—and the impact of that scene will convince the reader to delve further into the tale, hoping for more.

The Inciting Incident

An inciting incident is something that happens in a tale to start a story off. It's the major incident that occurs which lets us know a story has begun and our character has a problem to resolve.

In most stories, the inciting incident isn't revealed until after a few pages, usually ten to twenty in a novel, or at the end of the first 8 minutes in a movie.

Building up to that inciting incident may be the entire point behind the opening of your novel.

One really neat piece of advice I heard recently from an author goes like this: Have your characters make their own problems. In other words, it is interesting for a man to be standing outside and get hit by a falling branch. It creates a problem, but it's not much of a problem. Instead, what if the man is sitting in a tree, sawing off the limb upon which he is sitting?

Which would you rather read about?"

You see, if a person has something happen to him out of the blue, it may pose a problem for the character, but it's a simple problem, possibly one that is out of his control. If a branch falls on him, he has to get medical help. He will either live or die.

But if a person is at the root of his own problem, it hints at secondary problems—internal conflicts. The person who saws a limb off beneath himself is either suicidal or foolish – or perhaps so preoccupied with other problems that he doesn't realize what he is doing. In any case, he still has to deal with his injury while probing the root cause of his problem.

For a similar reason, a villain becomes just as interesting. If your character has a limb fall on him and discovers that it was some sort of a trap, he now has to deal with his injury – but he also has to wonder if the villain will strike again. He has to wonder at the villain's motivations and designs, and he may eventually have to come to blows.

In short, the least interesting of all conflicts tend to be those man-versus-nature conflicts where no human agency is involved.

Bridging Conflicts

As you are building up to reveal your inciting incident, you have to keep the reader's attention. Very often, that means that you have to have create bridging conflicts to interest the reader until you reach that big, overwhelming conflict.

So, for example, you might start a story with your protagonist arguing with a neighbor. We can learn from it that he is a good-hearted man, but he won't back down from a fight. We then follow him to the police station, where we discover that he is a detective, and find that his boss suspects that he stole some loot from the evidence locker. This points to the fact that he really does have a major financial crisis in the works. He's flat busted.

We then move on to discover that his sister has cancer, and he has spent all of his money on a radical new gene therapy that doesn't seem to be curing the cancer, even though the doctor promised that it would.

Until he's approached by a mysterious and attractive woman, one who is also ill, and who has given her life savings to the doctor—with no results. Only then does the detective begin to suspect that the good doctor is in fact a fraud, stealing money from his victims. Meanwhile, a German doctor working in the same field is having excellent results.

So that at last we reach a climax where the detective decides that he's going to "take it all back," get the victim's money from the evil doctor—but he has to do it in time to save his sister, and hopefully the other victims of the fraud.

Do you see how this last paragraph becomes the guiding influence for the whole tale? The previous smaller conflicts may only help lead us up to and introduce us to this inciting incident.

STORY MIDDLES

It has been said that there are three keys to creating great plots: escalate, escalate, escalate!

How exactly does a story get that satisfactory sense of "rising action" that Aristotle talked about? Here are a few tips....

Build on Rooting Interest

Your reader will only care about your story so long as he or she has rooting interest in your characters. Your job early in your story is to create characters that your reader will care about. This doesn't mean that you have to make "likable characters," people who are flawless, beautiful, well-educated and decent to the bone. Instead, we tend to root for characters who are perfectly fit for their role in life. Let me give you an example. Watch the movie *Casino Royale*. In it, James Bond is portrayed as a sociopathic killer. He's cunning, but he's not the most calculating man in the world. Instead, he's ruthless and he's obsessed with winning. He doesn't want to hunt down the enemy because they're evil, he wants to kill them because they are competition. In short, in most stories, James Bond would be the ultimate villain. Yet in this role, we buy off on him as the hero. How much rooting interest would *Casino Royale*'s James Bond have if you moved him into the role of a Catholic priest, or a suitor in a love triangle? The answer is none. And so as you create characters, as you begin considering how to create rooting interest, consider well what kind of character traits would seem admirable for a given protagonist within the environment of your story.

Remember that just as we can escalate the action of a story, we can also escalate the rooting interest in our characters. Some characters become more likeable, more noble, as we read on. So in order to make a character more likeable, we sometimes have to look at the protagonist and consider ways to surprise the reader.

In other words, let your character grow into the role of being the hero of his or her own story.

Just as a protagonist can become more likeable, a villain can also sink to deeper and deeper levels. He can have a chance at redemption, and choose not to take it.

Actions Speak Louder than Thoughts

You can't escalate the tension in your story if there isn't any to start with.

Far too often, stories start with a protagonist sitting on a rock, a couch, or on a bar stool furiously pondering a problem.

As an editor, I normally reject such stories immediately. The problem is that the author hasn't figured out this basic premise: when trying to solve a problem, thinking about it is weak.

The reason is that there is so little potential for conflict. So here is the rule: thinking about a problem is weaker than talking about it, and talking is weaker than taking action.

When your character is merely thinking about a problem, the tension tends to be minimal. Your protagonist might be confused about how to resolve the problem, but the truth is that he won't face any negative consequences for just thinking.

For example, let's say that he needs money desperately. He might think, "Okay, I'll empty my retirement savings." When he thinks that, what's the worst that can happen? He might argue with himself and say, "But if I do that, who will take care of me when I grow old?" Well, the truth is that he may have to work hard to make up for it later. That's weak.

But now imagine that he desperately needs money and he tells his wife, "I'm going to empty our retirement savings." His wife might answer, "I've been meaning to talk to you about that. I already emptied the savings. I spent it on meth." Or she might say, "That money is half mine. You even try to touch it, and I'm leaving you." I think you can see that an external argument, one that involves another person our protagonist cares about, is far more interesting than a mere internal argument.

And of course we can move it up a notch from there. Instead of starting with your character arguing with his wife about finances, you can start your story with him going to empty out his retirement account at the bank, demanding all $112,000—only to have a teller say, "I'm sorry sir, but your wife drained the last from this account on Monday." Now of course you have a mystery—"Why would my wife do that?"

So now his financial problems have gone from desperate to ruinous inside the space of a paragraph. Hence, by starting your story with action, as opposed to internal thought or an external conversation, you set a high bar for the following scenes in your story.

It is of course important to note that you will often have to have scenes where your characters are plotting both internally and with others on how to resolve problems. I've found that whenever possible, it helps to take those "plotting scenes" from internal argument, where your character is thinking, to an external argument, where two or more characters are actually arguing about how to resolve the problem. And of course, cut to action as soon as possible.

Make Problems Progressively more Difficult

As you move from your first try/fail cycle to your second, from your second to your third, and so forth, you must realize that your character's steps to resolve the problem should be progressively more difficult. By that, I mean that each attempt to resolve a problem should require greater effort and resources from your hero, and each attempt should also require you as an author to spend more time creating the scenes than the previous attempt.

Let's say, for example, that you start out writing a story about a serial killer. In the opening scene, the prologue, a young girl has been tied to a stone altar in the mountains, and a sadistic killer in black pulls out a knife and begins cutting off her clothes. The girl is terrified, and of course since you've been reading Orson Scott Card's book on character and viewpoint, you realize that this story must be told from her P.O.V., since she is in the most pain. But as the girl cries and pleads, you realize that there is something wrong. She begs the killer to leave her clothes on, apparently unaware that he intends to kill her. "Mommy says I'm not supposed to get naked. Don't make me naked," she cries. Suddenly you realize that though this girl is physically mature, she's not mentally all there. She's autistic. Of course the sadistic killer does what he will, and begins using his knife to cut a pentagram into the girl's chest.

We then go to our protagonist in chapter one—a detective who studies the crime scene. Thirteen-year-old girl, tortured and murdered—a human sacrifice made to Satan. For some people it might just be another case, but for this detective it's not. He has a daughter the same age. She's autistic, too.

Later that day, the case makes the news. Dad doesn't expect his daughter to even notice. She's usually too busy with her video games. But when the dead girl's picture flashes on the screen, she gives a startled cry. "It's Lizzy!" she yells, "It's Lizzy, from summer camp!"

Suddenly dad finds that there is a greater connection than he expected. His daughter goes to a summer camp for autistic girls, a place that is special and dear to her because there she meets with others who have similar problems. It's the only place she has ever been where she fits in, where she has true friends.

So our detective does all that he can to find the killer, but comes up with only a few leads. His failure devastates him.

This might end our first try/fail cycle. Let's say that it takes a hundred pages to get through, what with setting up the major characters and conflicts.

Now we get into the second try/fail cycle. Two weeks later, a second girl is found dead. This time, it's the governor's daughter. Once again, it's an autistic girl—one who went to his daughter's camp. In fact, he discovers that Lizzy and this new victim both shared a cabin with his daughter.

We can easily see that this story has taken on some new dimensions. Earlier, the fact that the girl was autistic might have been a coincidence. Now it appears that a pattern is developing. So our detective goes to the camp and searches the records. Two hundred girls went to that camp. Ten girls stayed in each cabin. Is it a counselor from the camp who is killing them? Is it one of the family members? Who would target autistic girls? Suddenly there are a lot more leads, of course. He has 200 families to interview, 30 camp counselors. From that list, he gleans half a dozen suspects.

This try/fail cycle will take longer to deal with, of course. Give yourself a good 150 to 200 pages.

Deepen and Broaden Your Tale

Notice that in this second try/fail cycle, the problem escalates. Often we say that the conflict "deepens" or "broadens." A conflict that deepens is one that becomes more personal to your protagonist, one that strikes closer to home. This one deepens in that the detective finds that someone is targeting girls like his daughter. It also deepens because, as he looks closer, he discovers that girls who were only names to him were best friends to her. Sure, he'd never even met them, but he finds that among his daughters' treasured pictures from camp, the three were always pictured together—riding horses, finger-painting, celebrating a birthday party. It gives our detective a very bad feeling. More than that, the governor is now going to be exerting pressure from all sides. New detectives will be brought to the case, though of course our guy will be left in charge.

But this story also "broadens." A conflict that broadens is one that begins to touch more and more lives as the story grows. In the opening, it seemed to be about one autistic girl. By the second murder, it has become something much larger. It's the kind of thing that would attract national media attention.

So while our detective is out hunting down leads, he suddenly learns that his own daughter did not return home from school. He know from the past MOs that the killer abducted both of his previous victims in the afternoon, cut pentagrams into them by moonlight, and plunged a knife into their hearts by midnight. He checks his watch. He suddenly realizes that he has seven hours to find rescue his daughter.

Do you think you'll handle that resolution in 50 pages? Of course not. He's going to look for her for at least a hundred. He'll figure out who the killer is and where the sacrifice is taking place in another 50, a raging battle with guns, and sacrificial knives might take another 50, and of course we'll need a good 20 for a resolution. By the time that you look at it, working toward and creating your final resolution might well make up 50 percent of your book.

In other words, with each major attempt at resolving this conflict, our protagonist must devote more effort and resources toward fixing the problem. The problem must grow in dimensions with each attempt—broadening and deepening. And you as an author must devote more and more resources toward creating a greater sense of jeopardy for the reader.

ENDING YOUR STORY WELL

Most new writers don't have a problem ending their story. After all, if you're working on a large novel and you've spent a year or two of your life working toward the ending, the chances are excellent that you've had a long time to ponder the ending, to weigh the possibilities, and to devise an ending that works for you.

But the resolution of a novel can be a very personal thing. A dozen years ago, Andre Norton was a judge for the Writers of The Future Contest. She was a wonderful person, a gracious judge, and an inspiration to those who met her. But she and I had some fundamental differences of opinion about what should happen at the ending of a story.

There is an old school of thought that goes like this: For any story to have a satisfying ending, the protagonist of the story must end up in a better, happier state than he or she began the story in.

Given this hypothesis, if your protagonist is single and desperately is looking for companionship, he or she needs to hear wedding bells before the novel closes. If the protagonist needs money, there had best be a fat wad of cash at the end of the rainbow.

Forgive me, but that doesn't always work for me. Oh, it can be gratifying. We all love to see deserving people succeed (or at least I hope we all do).

But I remember some of the movies that hit me the hardest on an emotional level, and they didn't all end that way.

When you boil a story down to its fundamentals, an ending is nothing more than a series of conflict resolutions. You might have some interesting plot twists and reversals in the end, and you can affect any kind of tone you want, from light-hearted banter to high seriousness, but the truth is that as an audience we are very curious to see how your story turns out.

Now, in a given novel we don't have just one protagonist. We might have four or five or more. We don't have just one antagonist, either. Every dark lord has his minions.

And with any given character, you might have a dozen conflicts that are brought up through the course of your story. Some may deal with life-and-death issues, while others touch on matters of the heart. Some of your conflicts might require your characters to grow, and some might be only simple philosophical arguments that your characters carry out on their back porch as they try to make sense of the world.

So your job as a writer is to find a resolution to nearly all of the conflicts.

Conflict Resolutions

As you create your conflicts throughout the beginning and middle of your story, you will of course grasp for the most interesting conflicts that you can. You will of course have your characters make brilliant attempts to resolve those conflicts, even if they fail miserably. In fact, they need to fail miserably at times. Great conflicts should never be resolved too easily.

And of course, in the end, you want your resolution to be as poignant as possible, so you'll consider all possible endings with an eye toward choosing the most emotionally powerful and satisfying ending available.

Want to know the secret to selecting a good ending? Here it is. With any given main storyline, only three things can arise out of your conflict:

—*Characters May Affect Change*: Your character may change his situation, his environment, and thus put an end to the conflict. This is the classic tale of the boy overcoming cancer, the hero putting down a mutiny, the cop catching the bad guy and blowing his brains out, the farm girl marrying the handsome landowner, and so on.

—*Characters May Change as a Result of Conflict*: In this ending, our protagonist is permitted to lose, so long as he or she grows from it. So the kid dies from cancer, but learns to grow and accept death in the process. Or your hero walks the plank, loses his ship, but is better prepared for the signs next time a mutiny is about to break out. In these cases, the growth of the character becomes more important than winning. Even though the battle is lost, something is salvaged from the incident. A good example of this is the movie *Rocky*. In the story, Rocky ultimately loses his battle royal with Apollo Creed, but in the process he gains some self-respect and, most importantly, begins learning how to really live.

—*Your Audience Can Be Changed by the Story*: Have you seen the movie *The Elephant Man*? As a college student, I had a roommate who could not abide the presence of people who were ugly, disabled, or otherwise impaired—losers—as he called them. Then one night for film class he was forced to watch *The Elephant Man*. After he came home that night, he wept freely for hours, and over the next several days he continued to weep bitter tears. The film dramatically changed him, helping him become a far more compassionate person. Years later, while working in Hollywood, I had dinner with the line producer on a few occasions who had cut his teeth on that film. In the intervening years he has worked on a number of huge Hollywood films with budgets that exceed $100 million films like *Hellboy*, the *Mission Impossible* movies, and so on—but I was impressed that of all the films he had made, *Elephant Man* was the most satisfying, and it was the kind of film that he yearned to make over and over again: films that change the world. Perhaps each of you can dig back into your own lives and find books or movies that have dramatically affected you.

So, your story can deeply affect the audience, even if your protagonist wins nothing, or salvages nothing.

But for me, I think there is a key to creating a great ending, the most powerful ending possible to your tale: the key is to consider how you might simultaneously do all three of the above. Write a story where a battle is won, but much is lost. (In real life, no one wins all of their battles, do they?) Write the story where your characters grow. (Or perhaps your reader only wishes they would grow; I'm thinking of the wonderful film *Remains of the Day*, a romance where loyalty interferes with love.) And, whenever possible, write a story that changes the hearts of your readers for good.

There are some rather famous tales that I think did all three for me. In Dickens's *A Christmas Carol*, Scrooge wins his battle against selfishness, is a changed man, and we are all changed with him—or at least I find myself giving uncharacteristically large donations to the needy if I happen to catch the play at Christmas. Tolkien does it in *The Lord of the Rings*. Frank Kapra did it for me in *It's a Wonderful Life*, and of course I could cite dozens of less-notorious examples of movies and films that worked for me.

Look at truly great stories and you will see this pattern emerge: The author often pulls off a complex resolution rather than working toward a simple resolution.

WRITING A MILLION DOLLAR OUTLINE

Over the years, I've seen a few articles about how to outline a book. All of them have been rather basic and tiring. Yet it's a skill that you need to develop. Here's why: For many books you will not want to write them on spec, but instead will hope to sell them on outline. This is true of authors who have published a couple of novels. Indeed, once your publisher knows you can write decent prose consistently, you probably will dispense with writing books on spec. So it becomes more important for older authors to learn how to write a great outline. The better your novel proposal looks, the more likely you are to be paid well for it.

I know of one author who took an outline for a novel to his agent, who then put it up for auction. When the bidding got into the millions of dollars, the publishers had to call a stop to the negotiations and ask for a new, extended outline—one that ran hundreds of pages long. Eventually the book sold for more than $4million dollars, but only after the outline itself was nearly 300 pages long.

Similarly, if you are going to write novelizations for movies, it can be lucrative work. For example, I've been paid more than $350,000 for my *Star Wars* novel *The Courtship of Princess Leia*, and I still make a few hundred dollars per month on royalties from it. The novel itself took less than four months to write, but writing it allowed me to work full time on other projects for years. Similarly, I've made hundreds of thousands of dollars writing on other projects, including young adult novels for *Star Wars*, *The Mummy*, various video games, and movie proposals. But if you want to get this kind of work, you will need to write from an outline that you create. That's because larger corporations will want to be sure that they like your ideas before they invest in your work.

This means you need to learn to outline well.

I'm not going to outline a book for you here, but I will go through the process.

Step 1: Lock Down Your Settings

Your character grows in part from your setting. A man living in China in 1600 has much different chances for an education than a man today. Also, a person's economic level, social status, and history are all dependent on setting.

Step 2: Identify Your Main Characters

Your main characters in a story include everyone the story is about—anyone whom you will follow through the story. Examples might be your protagonist, the girl he falls in love with, any buddies, sidekicks, or other helpers, the antagonist, the antagonist's minions, the love interest's friends, and so on. In short, a main character for the novel will include anyone who either participates in the story or is the focus of his or her own story.

Now, in my big fantasy novels, I often have three or more viewpoint characters, so each of those is a separate main character.

As I identify the characters, I might well begin to develop them, creating their backgrounds, habits, and so on.

Step 3: Identify Your Main Conflicts

I sometimes graph out a plot chart for each major character, and on that chart I decide what conflicts will figure into the story. For example, let's assume that my protagonist is a police detective. His main conflict might be, "Reginald must catch a serial killer—before the killer strikes at his own daughter." This might be the over-arching structure for my novel, but it isn't the only conflict that we'll have.

A good novel will have many conflicts. For example, in the story above one of my conflicts might include a romance angle where my detective falls in love with a wife of one of the killer's victims. Another minor conflict may have to do with his boss, a police chief who is so worn out that he no longer gives a damn about the job.

In fact, I will want a number of types of conflicts. My main conflict as stated above has to do with man vs. man, but there are other types of conflicts: man vs. self, man vs. society, man vs. nature, man vs. god.

For example, let's say I want to develop an internal conflict—man vs. self—in the story above. It may be that my main protagonist realizes that the serial killer is actually targeting child molesters—and as a young man, he himself was attacked. His own rage against the molesters might be so great, that secretly he wants to cheer the killer on—not apprehend him. So now we've added an internal conflict.

Another type is a conflict of "man vs. society." So let's give him one. Let's say he's looking for a killer of child molesters, but in a society that hinders him. Polygamists are in the news, so perhaps one of the victims is a polygamist— a man who has three wives, all of whom are under the age of 16. This is a closed society, and the women of course can't even admit that they're plural wives. Thus, in trying to identify the cause of the polygamist's murder, our detective finds that the polygamists in the compound are hampering him at every turn.

Conflicts might be small things—man versus nature. So you could throw one of these in, just to see how it affects the tale. Perhaps the entire story takes place during a snowstorm. Or what if the detective's gun has problems, and tends to misfire?

In short, I tend to think about my character's conflicts for a long time, adding conflict to conflict, until the story feels as if it is growing, gaining substance.

Step 4: Identify Conflicts for each of Your Characters.

By this I mean, when we are plotting novels we often have a tendency to forget that minor characters have conflicts, too. In particular, villains are often under-developed, along with the non-P.O.V. characters.

So I take each character and try to create a few juicy conflicts for them. For example, I might give my detective a secretary who is secretly in love with him. She grows jealous as he begins to fall for one of the dead polygamist's wives— so jealous that she decides not to tell him about an urgent phone call that he has received at the climax of the novel. I might want to round this woman out by giving her a mother who is dying from lung cancer, or a car that keeps breaking down.

It will become obvious to you as you begin to plot, that your conflicts begin to become interwoven.

For example, with your villain, it might be that there is a pesky detective trailing him—someone who comes to his home and questions him. So he discovers that he is a suspect. Suddenly your villain is your detective's main problem while the detective is your villain's biggest headache.

When you have two characters intertwined this way, your story will take on tremendous power. It's called "creating circuitry." Ideally, your hero and your villain will have circuitry, but your hero and his romantic interest might have it, too. In fact, if you create a love triangle, the villain and the heroine might have their own circuitry.

Just as you must create the conflicts for your hero and villain, if you have a love interest, your heroine will have to discover that she is in love, and this itself will create opportunities for troubles. In this case, we have a woman in a polygamous marriage. She might fall in love with your detective, but what will she do? She would have to turn her back on her religion to join him. She'd have to leave the compound that she was raised in and adopt the ways of the world. That would be hard to do in any case—but it's even harder in a snowstorm. Leaving the compound would be to commit spiritual suicide.

Even if she does decide to go, she has to wonder if the detective could really accept her, really love her as a woman. After all, she is only 16!

As I create these conflicts, I sometimes will see opportunities to begin plotting. In short, I'll see that there might be try/fail cycles that comes to mind. I like to take a clean piece of paper and graph the conflicts for each character separately. Ideally I like to spend a day or so at the task, just thinking of cool ways to make the conflict lines work together, build on each other.

Step 5: Embellish on the Conflicts by Brainstorming how Your Characters will try to Resolve them.

Every story consists of a character with a problem, and deals with his attempts to resolve that problem.

This happens in several phases. In phase 1, the character recognizes that he has a problem—a big problem, one that will change his life.

In phase 2, the character tries to resolve the problem and fails. As a result, the problem grows or escalates. It might deepen, meaning that the problem will have a more powerful affect on the character. For example, our detective begins to investigate a murder and thinks at first that it is just another case. He might even try to laugh it off—after all, it was just some dumb polygamist that got killed. But as he begins to get involved, he becomes more absorbed by the problem. Perhaps he has trouble sleeping, or he can't stop thinking about the polygamist's wife. His desire to help her becomes overwhelming. His own internal demons start to surface, and he fears going mad—that's what we mean when we say that the problem deepens.

But the problem could also broaden, meaning that it will affect more people. For example, as the investigation continues, our detective discovers the same killer has targeted several other people, and as our detective closes in, he suddenly has reason to suspect that the killer (who feels that he has been robbed of a victim), decides to strike at the detective's own family.

Sometimes the problem can become both deeper and broader. In fact, in the best stories, both will happen. But just remember, you have to find ways to escalate the stakes.

Each time a character tries to resolve a problem, escalate, escalate, escalate.

In phase 3 of each plot chart, the character attempts to resolve his problems. Along the way, he will discover that he has to work harder than he imagined. He'll have to struggle, draw upon reserves of strength and cunning he didn't know that he had. And he must fail to resolve the problem a second time, a third, and possibly even a fourth time.

In phase 4, the character finally discovers a solution to the problem, and must face it head-on. This means that if the detective is confronting a killer, he will have to deal with him—typically one-on-one, in a desperate moment.

So, with all of this in mind, I begin looking closely at my conflicts and begin brainstorming scenes in which my character will try to resolve the conflicts. For example, if he's trying to stop a murderer, I might have a scene where he goes to question the killer. Our detective might have a strong suspicion, but he's looking for proof. So I have to figure out how the killer will elude him.

On the other hand, if I am dealing with a romance angle, I'd have to create a scene where the detective finds himself falling in love with the 16-year-old widow to a polygamist. I'd have to wonder, what character strengths will she convey that could make him love her? I might imagine ways that he could try to approach her, to court her, and so on.

I now do this with every single conflict in my tale.

I don't have to develop a full plot structure for each conflict. It might be that a conflict doesn't require it. For example, I might decide that at one time, our detective takes a shot at a fleeing suspect—a shadowy figure leaving the scene of a murder—and his gun jams. So he goes home that night and files the action down, so that not only will it not jam, it now has a hair-trigger. So the conflict here is resolved with only one attempt on the detective's part, but it is a significant action and therefore needs to be concluded.

These are my first steps in creating my outline—simply deciding what conflicts I'll have and what resolution attempts I might try.

You'll notice that I don't have an outline quite yet. I don't know exactly what scenes will take place, or what order they'll come in. That is all yet to be determined.

But I am beginning to let my story take shape.

Step 6: Merging Characters onto a Plot Chart

By now, you should have gone through your main characters and created basic conflicts, writing each step of your try/fail cycles onto a sheet of paper. These character sheets should have a nice mix of problems—everything from taking a Ring of Doom to the into the Dark Lord's domain, to fleeing Ring Wraiths, to fighting off your best friends and supporters—down to the deepest internal conflicts.

At this point, if I'm working on a complex outline, I go down to an office supply store and buy me some paper. This might be poster board, or a white board, or something like that. I usually look for something that is about two feet by three feet at the very least. And I want some color markers— a different color for each character.

Then I go home and I lay all of my major characters' conflict charts out in front of me, and I read through them one last time. At this point, I plot out the novel on a standard plot chart. I then draw out the protagonist's main plot using a heavy solid line.

But wait a minute—a story doesn't have just one "plot line" in the way that teacher's in writing classes like to show you.

No, each different conflict has its own plot line. So I need to consider where in the novel the various plot lines for each character are going to come. I might have a romance line in the same color (let's say green), but I distinguish it from the main plot by making long dashed lines. If I have a third conflict—let's say that my hero has an issue with fear of his father that he needs to overcome—then I plot out the incidents that must come about for that conflict to be properly resolved, and maybe I'll do those with short dashes.

Thus, I need to plot out each conflict on my paper, making sure that I include the try/fail cycles, climaxes, and resolutions for each conflict. In order to keep them straight, I'll also write a little tag at the beginning of each conflict line.

What you should get when you try this is SEVERAL plot lines for your protagonist, showing where the peaks and troughs will come into play over the timeline of your novel.

Now, your character doesn't act in isolation. If you're following multiple characters through your story, you need to go through and outline each of their conflicts, and these will all interconnect. Thus, when your villain has a run-in with your detective, for example, if your villain wins a round in their battle, then while your detective is out getting drunk in an effort to kill the pain, the villain might be sitting two stools down at the bar celebrating his good fortune.

So what you're interested in here is creating something of a dance of plots. You can write scenes where a great deal is happening at once—to five different characters, so that everyone is hitting a peak at the same time. This will affect your reader powerfully.

But you can't have everyone peaking all of the time.

You need, instead, to make sure that there is plenty of action, that your characters are working and struggling. You don't want to have dead zones where no one is doing anything.

So you look at your plot chart and make sure you don't have any long stretches where none of your characters seems to have much going on. If you study your protagonist's main plot line, then compare the main plot with all of the other characters, you should have something of a "sawtooth" effect of different lines rising and falling all along the primary plot line. Each of those rises and falls represents scenes that you'll add into your book.

Now, I find that the first third of the book is where I tend to find slow sections.

That's because when you're writing a novel, you spend a great deal of time introducing the characters and the world in the first third of the book, and so we tend to allow ourselves as writers a bit too much time to get things going. So if I find a slow section, I have to figure out ways to hold my readers' interest.

This might mean that I need to adjust a character's plot line in some way. For example, let's say that I have a subplot that deals with a love interest. If I find that I've got a dull spot, then I'll try to move that love story—or some other inner conflict—up into position to create more motion in the story.

You may find as you do this that you're juggling too many conflicts. By this I mean that as you look at the totality of your story, you may discover that you've got excellent movement throughout the tale—as shown by lots of seesaw lines along the main plot trajectory. So I've been known to look at the shape of my story and say, "You know, I've got too much going on. I'll just eliminate one." If you do, that's okay.

Now, the problem that you might have when you first try doing this is that you have difficulty looking at the "shape" of the story as depicted on a graph and equating it with the linear story that you put on paper.

When you first begin trying to outline, you often don't have enough experience writing so that you can tell where your outline has gone bad. But if you're writing, and it feels like the story has become a bit sluggish, then you'll be able to look at your outline and go, "Aha, I should have seen that this problem would arise."

In short, you learn how to write from an outline gradually, by trying it out a few times. Once you learn the skill, of course, you'll begin to see how great it is as a tool. Eventually, you'll discover that you have an ideal story shape in your head—one that appeals to you more than any other. At least, I know that I do. So I've become fairly adept at looking at the shape of a tale in an outline and then recognizing how well it will work as a story.

(As a side note, over the years I've come to the point where I sometimes dream about story shapes in three dimensions. I've heard that other writers eventually do this, too.)

So, your next step is to merge all of your story lines for your major characters into one massive plot chart.

Now, this is very important: If you are writing from the points of view of two or more characters, you're going to need to make sure that your high points, your complication for each conflict, are staggered in such a way so you can keep track of whose P.O.V. you're in. By this I mean, let's say that you're following the stories of two love-birds, Dan and Diane, and you're going to write in alternating chapters with Dan's P.O.V. first. You'll need to make Dan's outline for their major moments is staggered slightly behind Diane's, so that you're adjusting for the lag that it takes to tell the story for that character.

Once you've done this, you're ready to move on to the next step in creating your outline—writing it out on paper in a scene by scene, chapter by chapter format.

One final note: I know some authors prefer to create plot points on 3x5 cards. If you use colored cards, you can use a different color for each character, or perhaps for each type of conflict. These cards can then be arranged later, much as we are arranging the plot points on our chart. Both ways can work fine.

Step 7: Turn Your Giant Plot Chart into a Sequential Outline.

Once you've created your master plot chart, you begin writing your outline by taking each of your plot points and using it to become a scene or chapter.

I like to sit down and just begin writing descriptive paragraphs of what happens at each plot point.

This should all still be a very creative process. In other words, you've figured out the basic shape of your story. You've put a lot of creative energy up to this point just figuring out what your story line is going to be. But when you begin brainstorming your chapters, you'll find that you're now concentrating on how to tell the story scene by scene.

Your goal in writing each chapter is simple. You want to move toward having a decent-sized "change" in every chapter. Now, a change implies some sort of motion. Perhaps the change is momentous—your detective goes to a hotel room to question a suspect, and a gunman shoots through the door, hits him, and leaves him for dead. But sometimes the change is much smaller. Perhaps the change is all emotional—your heroine decides that she likes this detective, enough to smile next time that she sees him.

As you write your chapters, try to be economical. Try to create scenes that accomplish more than one thing. I used to have a writing teacher in college who said that he wouldn't write a chapter that didn't accomplish at least three things. So perhaps you can merge the two scenes above into one, for example. You'll find that if a writer typically only tries to accomplish one plot movement per chapter, his or her work will feel rather weak.

So, you describe each and every plot point.

I always start out by naming my point-of-view character for that chapter, the location, and often the time of day. Thus, I might say, "Sir Borenson is picking apples with his daughter Sage (age 14) and Erin (age 12) in his orchard.…"

This might sound rather simple, but it helps keep track of things. You'll notice quickly if you have a character disappear, or if you're inserting too many "night scenes," or too many scenes set indoors or outdoors. If you're writing a story that you want to have turned into a movie, for example, you have to beware of trying to set too many shots at dawn or sunset. Such shots are notoriously difficult to film, for the moments are so fleeting.

The other thing I do is to associate the character's name with a color. Thus, in the outline for my current novel, Sir Borenson's color is blue. Any scene in my outline that he is in, I put in blue font. If I move to his wife, Myrrima, for a scene, I switch to her color—red. Villains are in black, and so on. The reason for doing this is simple. When I'm done with my outline, I'll be able to put the pieces of paper up on a wall and simply glance at the colors to make sure that my viewpoint characters don't drop out on me, or else appear too much.

Beyond the character and setting information, I go through and compose each scene in the chapter. I want to make sure I don't have too many internal scenes right in a row, where I'm just in the head of one character as he goes about an action. So, let's say I want to have Borenson do something. I ask myself, who else could appear with him in this chapter, or in this scene. It's especially valuable—from the point of view of economy, if I make sure my protagonists appear together as much as possible. It's just as important to make sure that my protagonists and antagonists meet frequently.

Thus in each chapter I might have between two and five separate scenes. I try to make sure that some of those are dialog-rich while others are action-intense and still others have powerful emotional impact.

As I compose this rough draft of my outline, I usually try to give at least a paragraph for each scene. I often separate these scenes with bullet points.

If there is any particular information that logically *must* be delivered in a particular scene, then I make sure to add that to the scene description. For example, if in chapter eight scene D my detective discovers that his gun is defective, and that becomes vital information in scene G, then I note where the information must go.

Your chapter-by-chapter outline is still something that you're brainstorming on. You may find as you consider the chapter that you have a great idea for an argument, or an especially juicy line. I like to throw those into my outline so I remember them when I'm writing the novel. In fact, I've had times where I've stopped in an outline to spend a couple of pages describing a tree, a building, or a character.

The question arises, how long should your outline be?

I've mentioned that if you want to sell a novel for a million dollars, the answer is that typically the outline may be detailed. However, some editors balk when they see such a huge document. It really depends upon the job.

For example, if I'm going to sell the fifth novel in a series and I've already sold the first four, I might not do more than give my editor a sentence of description about the novel—especially if this is a bestselling series. Similarly, if I'm writing a movie treatment, the rule of thumb is that it should be between ten and 20 pages. So I don't want a massive document in this case.

If I'm writing a document to sell the first book in a series, 20 pages is often considered quite adequate—but I've heard of some writers who always write 80 or 100 pages.

I've written outlines for my personal use that were 70 or 80 pages.

So don't be afraid to go long. Instead, focus on getting as much detail as possible on the chapter-by-chapter level.

Every writer does what we call "pre-writing." By this I mean we tend to spend a good amount of time staring off into space and daydreaming. Hopefully, you're not like me. I tend to do way too much of my daydreaming while I'm driving.

But I've found over the years that if you just sort of let it happen, if you just let yourself daydream about an upcoming novel, you'll probably spend days or weeks focusing on only a couple of scenes. So when you sit down to write you discover you've got lots of information but that it only covers relatively small portions of your novel.

Doing this exercise—outlining the novel as a whole—forces you to make a basic game plan for the entire book. As you do, you'll find yourself getting excited about scenes that you never even thought about writing before. So it can be exhilarating.

Step 8: Map the Flow of Emotions.

Now, this is something I do that no one else does (to my knowledge).Once I have written my outline scene by scene, I will often look through the story and make notations on the side of the outline, mapping the emotional flow of the piece.

There are a number of reasons I do this. First, as I've said before, we don't really write in "genres." Instead, we write in emotions. Thus, the romance market fulfills a reader's need for romance in her life. A thriller brings excitement to an otherwise boring life. A fantasy should deliver wonder.

So part of the reason I map emotions is to see if I'm hitting the right emotional highpoints for my market. In other words, if I'm selling "wonder" in my novel, I need to make sure I have enough scenes to elicit wonder.

But there are other reasons to map out your emotions. I consider my book to be a symphony of emotions. Just as a musician might strike a key on a piano, I strike emotional chords with my readers. I want to make sure I'm not hitting the same chord five times in a row.

So I look at the flow of my story. I might mark in the side of one paragraph: humor. But an instant later, a mystery comes into play, followed by a sense of danger, then to wonder.

Sometimes, if I want to heighten a particular emotion, I might purposely hit the same chords three or four times in a row, trying to create a more powerful emotional experience with each succeeding scene.

Finally, I want to make sure that some emotions aren't missing. For example, if you're writing a novel for the middle grades, you should know that one of the biggest draws is humor. So if you've written a novel for that age level and it is lacking in humor, then you might want to do a bit more brainstorming.

As I map emotions, I often insert notes on plotting tools that I might want to use in that chapter.

Step 9: Add Non-Plot Details.

Much that goes into your outline has little to do with the story. For example, you will need some minimal descriptions of your characters, and you might need to embellish your setting, too, adding such things as the weather, etc.

Beyond that, you need to make your story plausible. Now, a compelling story sometimes requires your character to do some extraordinary things. Your hero who is afraid of water might need to jump into a roaring river in order to save the woman he loves. So you'll need to explain to the reader of your outline why the character is doing what he or she is doing, which means that you need to explain the character's motives. You don't just say, "Leroy jumps into the foaming rapids."

But there are other non-plot details you might add. For example, we've talked about outlining the conflicts that are in your story, but not all conflicts result in a "story arc." Let's say that your character is ravenously hungry. He goes to the local hamburger shop and buys some fries. Problem solved.

That's obviously not a story. A story about a hungry person might go something like this: Your little pioneer girl is crossing the plains and the family's supplies are stolen by some Indians. So she starts looking for berries each day. One day she goes looking and doesn't find any. Desperate, she goes hunting farther and sees a rabbit. Picking up a sharp stick she tries to spear it and misses. Now, miles from camp, she finally finds some blackberry bushes with a few ripe berries. But as she's picking them, a black bear charges her. Terrified, the girl rams the sharpened stick into the bear's eye socket, puncturing its brain. Now, instead of berries, she eats the bear.

The above paragraph is a story arc—complete with two try/fail cycles, a climax, and an ending that contains a reversal.

So a story has an over-arching plot structure where the conflict drives the character to greater and greater extremes in an effort to resolve the problem—usually ending in a surprising or gratifying conclusion.

Yet, there will be many non-arc problems in your story. Maybe your detective needs to get to a meeting but can't find his car keys for a few minutes. Maybe he has a running fight with his wife through the whole book, but it is never resolved.

I prefer to add something unnecessary to a story rather than leave things out. Regardless of which method you choose, you can give the story some "rough edges" so it doesn't feel contrived.

Step 10: Write out a Final Draft of the Outline.

Now, at this point, I normally save my entire rough outline on my computer. Much of what I have in it might be personal notes or partial scene descriptions—information that I don't want to discard, nor do I want editors or agents seeing it.

So after saving it, I turn all of the text from its various colors back to black. I get rid of my marginal notes and my emotional tags and plotting tools, and here is the trick: at this point, I just rewrite my outline and briefly tell the story as powerfully as I can.

Of course, I tell what happens in present tense. Instead of saying, "John ran to the bomb site," I'll say, "John runs to the bomb site."

But you should do more than that. You'll want to insert lines of proposed dialog so that it helps with the pacing of your outline. Such quotes should be memorable or powerful.

Rather than writing a dry outline that just plods along telling what happens, I want to invest it with emotion. Characters may wonder what will happen. They might curse the fates. But whatever is going on, try to show those emotions.

Don't forget to try to write beautifully. This means that you'll have similes and metaphors in your outline. You'll pay attention to poetic details—the assonance and consonance in your words, the stresses on syllables, and so on.

Of course all of the skills that come to play in writing a fine novel are used in an outline. You'll write with economy and grace, using strong verbs, offering up gorgeous descriptions, and so on. I've seen Hollywood writers whose screenplays are works of art.

Most importantly, you want your editors to feel your story. A great outline ought to inspire him or her to laugh aloud at the jokes, to reach an emotional climax, and hopefully to weep in the end.

The goal of writing your "Million Dollar Outline" is to sell your publishers on the idea that this is a million-dollar novel.

Give it your best shot!

APPENDIX

TAKING A STORY FROM IDEA TO COMPLETION

Tips on Writing from an Outline

Writing from an outline may seem "easy" to a writer—and therein lies a danger. Many outline writers fall into bad habits, writing as if they were mere reporters, with thin characters, settings that don't seem realistic, and lackluster prose.

As a novelist, you have to rise above these hurdles. You want our tale to become as rich and powerful as it can be. By using an outline, you free yourself from worrying about "what will happen next" and allow yourself to focus on "how can I best bring this scene to life."

So you take your outline and use it to compose one scene at a time, putting your focus on telling the story well.

Never allow yourself to fall into a routine. When you're creating a character, you may need to draw from deep within your own well of personal experience and draw upon your imagination to bring that character to life—considering well how the character is dressed, what he or she thinks about, their recent history, and so on. But don't allow your characters to come to life so fully that they do the unexpected. You're the writer. You need to make sure that your characters serve the purpose of the story.

The same is true of your setting. You need to take time to fully create it. This means that you bring it to life using of all the senses—sight, sound, taste, feel, smell. It also means that you need to explore the nuances of your setting. When a character enters a restaurant, is there a table waiting for them, or does the waiter need to clear it? You may need to do some research to find out how your menu reads—let's say that it's a French restaurant in modern St. Petersburg. So you may need to go online, look at menus, perhaps even peruse travel books to find out what restaurant you want to use.

But the story that you're creating requires much more than just mere reportage. One powerful draw for readers will be your own personal voice and tone, and that of your characters. You need to be sensitive to how you use language. It isn't enough to just describe, you have to figure out how to entertain your readers with every sentence.

In short, there are pitfalls to relying too heavily upon the outline, with its great plot, to create a story. You need to learn to adopt the strengths of the tool, while avoiding those pitfalls.

Mystery Man on Indiana Jones Story Conference

We've talked about the plotting process. Here's an example of how it's done taken from a story conference long ago. You'll be familiar with the movie. It might be helpful to know that this story conference took more than a week, and included the input of some of the finest writers in the film industry:

Hey, guys, you're going to love this (and thanks, Viktor).

There is a **link** now available to download the 125-page transcript (in the form of a .pdf document) of the original 1978 story conference between Steven Spielberg, George Lucas, and Lawrence Kasdan for a little film called *Raiders of the Lost Ark*.

Some background first. Spielberg suggested that Kasdan write *Raiders* because he admired his *Continental Divide* script. Lucas agreed. Now, imagine with me: Lucas had just released *Star Wars*, the biggest film in the history of Hollywood and a cult phenomenon. Spielberg had just released *Close Encounters of the Third Kind* and before that, *Jaws*. Now Kasdan was called in to have a story conference with the biggest names in Hollywood who wanted to talk about their next blockbuster. The conference took place at the L.A. home of Jane Bay, who was Lucas' assistant. They had five consecutive 9-hour days to talk about the story. This .pdf is a transcript from taped recordings of those meetings.

By the time Lucas and Spielberg setup these meetings with Kasdan, they knew for the most part what they wanted. This was just a matter of "okay, so, how do we tell this story?" Lucas did most of the talking. He seemed to be just talking through all of the ideas. He came across as, on the one hand, a strong driving force behind the film and on the other hand, a bit controlling. Spielberg occasionally threw in some exciting, funny, and even wacky ideas, which at times Lucas tried to dial down. But many, if not most, of Spielberg's ideas would be used. Kasdan doesn't say too much. I imagine he's just soaking in everything he's hearing, but he was certainly in sync with the filmmakers. He'd occasionally interject suggestions and also good questions about logic, characters, and plot.

Man-oh-man, Spielberg and Lucas were idea machines. They could've sat there coming up with Indiana Smith ideas forever. There were enough ideas generated in these meetings for two films, which they actually used for two films. I must say, it's rather unusual to have meetings with a producer and a director and be given so many ideas. Not that meetings with producers and directors wouldn't have a lot of ideas but I'm not sure you would encounter such a volume as this. For screenwriters, it's a goldmine. If you try to forget the finished film and put yourself into Kasdan's shoes and you have all these ideas thrown at you, it can be a daunting task. What do you keep? What do you throw away? How do you make all this work?

In any case, there were about 10 Screenwriting Lessons I took away from this experience and thought they might be worth sharing.

Before they ever discussed the plot, they figured out who and what their hero-protagonist is and how he'd be similar and also different from other heroes in cinema.

The story began with the character, which was integral to the concept. So much was said that it's hard to condense, but here's a taste:

(Key: G = George; S = Steven; L = Larry)

G—The thing with this is, we want to make a very believable character. We want him to be extremely good at what he does, as is the Clint Eastwood character or the James Bond character. James Bond and the Man With No Name were very good at what they did. They were very fast with a gun. They were very slick. They were very professional. They were Supermen.

S—Like Mifune.

G—Yes, like Mifune. He's a real professional. He's really good. And that is the key to the whole thing. That's something you don't see that much anymore.

Later:

G—He's the guy who's been all around the world. He's a soldier of fortune. He is also.... Well, this gets into that other side of his character, which is totally alien to that side we just talked about. Essentially, I think he is a, and this was the original character and it's an interesting juxtaposition. He is an archeologist and an anthropologist. A Ph.D. He's a doctor, he's a college professor. What happened is, he's also a sort of rough and tumble guy. But he got involved in going in and getting antiquities. Sort of searching out antiquities. And it became a very lucrative profession so he, rather than be an archeologist, he became sort of an outlaw archeologist. He really started being a grave robber, for hire, is what it really came down to. And the museums would hire him to steal things out of tombs and stuff. Or, locate them. In the archeology circles he knows everybody, so he's sort of like a private detective grave robber. A museum will give him an assignment ... a bounty hunter.

Later:

G—I think basically he's very cynical about the whole thing. Maybe he thinks that most archeologists are just full of shit, and that somebody's going to rip this stuff off anyway. Better that he rips it off and gets it to a museum where people can study it and rip it off right. That's the key also. He knows how to enter a tomb without destroying it. He knows what's important. He knows not to go in there like a bull in a china shop and destroy half the stuff that's valuable.

And later:

G—It's such an odd juxtaposition, especially going around. The first sequence is in the jungle and you see him in action. You see him going through the whole thing. And the next sequence after that you see him back in Washington or New York, back in the museum. Where he's in a totally academic thing, turning over this thing that he's got. Then in the rest of the movie you see him back in his bullwhip mode. You understand that there's more to him. Plus, it

235

justifies later things that he… the fact that he's sort of an intelligent guy. Peter Falk is one way of looking at him, a Humphrey Bogart character. The fact that he's sort of scruffy and, not the right image, but…

S—Peter's too scruffy.

G—Yes. We'll figure a way of laying that out in his personality so it's easily identifiable.

S—Remember the movie Soldier Of Fortune *with Clark Gable? There was a good deal of Rhett Butler in that character. The devil-may-care kind of guy who can handle situations. He's so damn glib he bluffs everybody around. People think that he's a push-over. He's challenged, and he always appears like a push-over. But in fact he's not. He likes to set himself up in these subordinate roles from time to time to get his way.*

G—What I'm saying is that character just would not fit in a college classroom or even as an archeologist. He's too much of a scruffy character to settle down. A playboy, or however you want to do it. He's too much of a wise-guy, maybe that's a better way to say it, to actually be a college professor. He really loves the stuff, but he became too cynical, he's too much of a wise guy to fit into an academic situation, or even an archeological situation. He's really too much of an adventurer at heart. He just loves it. So he obviously took this whole bent that was different because it's just more fun. He just can't settle down. It's a nice contrast. It's like the James Bond thing. Instead of being a martini drinking cultured kind of sophisticate, he's the sort of intellectual college professor James Bond. He's a superagent.

S—Clark Kent.

G—Yeah. It's that thing, which is fun. It's the same idea, only twisted around a little bit….

On the name:

L—Do you have a name for this person?

G—I do for our leader.

S—I hate this, but go ahead.

G—Indiana Smith. It has to be unique. It's a character. Very Americana square. He was born in Indiana.

L—What does she call him? "Indy?"

G—That's what I was thinking. Or "Jones." Then people can call him "Jones."

A character arc? What's that?

There was also no discussion *about an arc*, and as you can see, they referenced characters that did not arc, such as James Bond, the Man With No Name, Superman, and some of Clark Gable's characters.

A racy backstory can keep a plot moving.

Interestingly, the discussion about Marion was hardly as thorough as the one about Indy. For a while, they weren't sure what kind of girl to have as a counterpart to Indy. Lucas had first described the love interest as a blonde double-crossing German agent, which they ended up using in Last Crusade. Spielberg said, "She should have hair like Veronica Lake. You only see one eye at a time."

There was talk about a big name professor who taught Indy everything he knew. Then there was the idea about this German girl, and for the sake of expediency, Kasdan suggested that Indy instead have an affair with the mentor's daughter, which they loved. And then Lucas and Spielberg were off and running with ideas about how's she's been left in Peru and has this bar and is trying to get money together to get back to the States and loves (and resents) Indy to no end. In fact, Kasdan said he wanted Indy and this girl to already have a history when they meet because, "I like it if they already had a relationship at one point. Because then you don't have to build it." Hehehe…

Then the discussion turned to how old Marion and Indy were at the time of the affair:

G—I was thinking that this old guy could have been his mentor. He could have known this little girl when she was just a kid. Had an affair with her when she was eleven.

L—And he was forty-two.

G—He hasn't seen her in twelve years. Now she's twenty-two. It's a real strange relationship.

S—She had better be older than twenty-two.

G—He's thirty-five, and he knew her ten years ago when he was twenty-five and she was only twelve. It would be amusing to make her slightly young at the time.

S—And promiscuous. She came onto him.

G—Fifteen is right on the edge. I know it's an outrageous idea, but it is interesting. Once she's sixteen or seventeen it's not interesting anymore. But if she was fifteen and he was twenty-five and they actually had an affair the last time they met. And she was madly in love with him and he…

S—She has pictures of him.

And now consider the dialog of that scene in the film:

INDY: I never meant to hurt you.

MARION: I was a child! I was in love.

INDY: You knew what you were doing.

MARION: It was wrong. You knew it.

INDY: Look, I did what I did. I don't expect you to be happy about it. But maybe we can do each other some good.

MARION: Why start now?

INDY: Shut up and listen for a second. I want that piece your father had. I've got money.

MARION: How much?

Consider the debate about unsympathetic protagonists.

At one point, they figured out that he'd go to Marion to get a pendant thingee, a puzzle of some kind that her father collected and will help Indy find the Ark. But she doesn't want to give it to him. And she goes with him on this adventure. So then the question became, how does he get this thing from Marion to solve the puzzle?

They tossed around an idea about him stealing the pendant from her, which prompted a short debate about unsympathetic protags:

G—It would be nice if they left in a huff, they fought or something. He left rather pissed. I don't think he would leave without the pendant. That's the only thing that bothers me about that.

S—So he goes upstairs and stays up, plotting how he's going to take it off her.

G—That makes him into a real rat.

L—That's all right. He never does it. What he does is just the opposite, save her life.

G—No matter how you do it, the fact that he thought about it is the rat part.

S—Rhett Butler was a rat.

G—He wasn't a real rat—

S—He proved himself by raising her family. Before that he was a gambler, dealt with cheap ladies.

G—There's a difference between being a rat and somebody who's having fun. He never hurt anybody.

L—I'm a little confused about Indiana at this point. I thought he'd do anything for this pendant.

G—But he still has to have some moral scruples. He has to be a person we can look up to. We're doing a role model for little kids, so we have to be careful. We need someone who's honest, trusting and true. But at the same time he's confronted with this difficult problem. We have a great thing when she won't give it to him. She doesn't like him.

L—What if you see them separate, and you see them both thinking about it, and it's clear that she's going to give it to him. Then he saves her and she doubts his motivation, was he coming to steal it? Or was he coming to rekindle the romance? It doesn't have to be crystal clear to her.

Interesting to me that they didn't have a debate about unsympathetic protags when they were talking about Indy having an affair with the underage daughter of his mentor. That builds sympathy how? But they're terribly concerned about losing sympathy if we might watch Indy consider stealing the pendant from Marion. (Also, here, Lucas and Spielberg were both projecting their own unique feelings onto Rhett Butler. Rhett *was* a cheating rat and he never once redeemed himself with that dysfunctional family he created. He spoiled the hell out of his wife and his little girl, which was in part why she died.)

However, I think there might be some screenwriting nuggets here. What happens in the past, off screen, good or bad, does not affect sympathy. It's what we see the character do in the present that determines how much we will or will not care about that character.

Consider how tension was always a high priority as they laid-out their plot for the film

The first scene was all about building the tension to a big payoff, which was a boulder as Spielberg suggested. But you had to set that up first and work your way backwards. So going backwards, you create tension with the near betrayal against Indy when he put the map together and had to use his whip on the man that pulled out the gun. You have the fresh poison darts of the Hovitos. You have his entourage not going any further when they reached the stone sculpture of a Chachapoyan demon. You have tarantulas. You have the dead competitor in the Chamber of Light. You have the pit. You have the dart floor in the Foyer of the Sanctuary. And then you have the big payoff to all the big danger that all of these details setup.

The consideration in Act Two was about maintaining tension. Here are highlights of comments George made…

G—People are trying to kill him as soon as he arrives or maybe even before he arrives on the airplane. As soon as he gets there, there are knives coming out of walls, all these slimy characters are following him, all that stuff that happens in those places in the thirties…

There's a lot of tension because we have established that everybody is trying to kill him. People are following him all over the place…

The idea in the middle sequence was to create sort of a race, tension, who's going to find the Ark first situation.

So much of the tension and gags was a matter of backtracking. Consider how Indy is finally underground in the temple. He found the Ark and had it hoisted up. At this stage of development, the temple was not full of snakes. The Germans grab the Ark and seal Indy inside to die. So what do you do with Indy then?

How do you raise the tension and suspense in this scene and also find a way for him to escape? They first decided that the temple be suddenly filled with water and Indy floated up to a place where he figured out how to escape. This idea could be setup with Indy entering a sand temple and there's moss on the walls. But will audiences believe that there could be so much underground water in a desert? Lucas suggested setting that up verbally by talking about an underground water system. Nah. How about filling the temple with sand? Nah. Then Spielberg suggested that the Germans lower hungry lions into the temple to kill Indy, which would give him the chance to use his bull whip. Nah. How about rats? Or how about snakes? Hundreds of thousands of snakes. It could be a giant snake pit.

And then they were off and running about the snakes in the temple.

S—It would be funny if, somewhere early in the movie he somehow implied that he was not afraid of snakes. Later you realize that that is one of his big fears.

G—Maybe it's better if you see early, maybe in the beginning that he's afraid: "Oh God, I hate those snakes." It should be slightly amusing that he hates snakes, and then he opens this up, "I can't go down in there. Why did there have to be snakes? Anything but snakes." You can play it for comedy...

So then they go back to figure out when and how you can setup the snake joke in the opening sequence. A lot of screenwriting is backtracking, of setups and payoffs.

Consider their approach to exposition.

So Indy's in Cairo with his friend. We're at a scene that we know will be full of exposition, that is, the Staff of Ra was too long for the Germans and they're digging in the wrong place. So the question was, "what are we going to do to make the scene interesting so the audience doesn't fall asleep?" And the idea was presented that this exposition could be done over dinner that's been poisoned. As they pick up tainted food and gesture with it, we fear for their lives. They loved it. (And I've been saying this for years - great exposition is always given in the context of something else.) Okay, now that we have the setup, how do they figure out the food is poisoned and survive? A pet nibbles on it and dies. Okay, what kind of pet?

S—What if it's an animal we hate, an animal the audience can't stand. It's always after our hero and doesn't like him very much, like a mongoose.

G—A monkey is a perfect thing.

S—What animal don't people like?

G—A rat.

S—A pet rat.

G—It doesn't have to be a pet.

L—He's looking the other way, the rat comes up.

S—That's a pretty brave rat.

G—It wouldn't come on the table.

So then they're off and running about this pet monkey. Why is the monkey here? Is it a family pet? Maybe it just attaches itself to one of the characters and won't go away. Is it dressed up like a circus monkey? Perhaps it's secretly helping a German agent? Well, what kind of bad things can a monkey do for a German agent? It was hilarious. I was rolling. But ya know, figuring out those details is crucial to a script. Finally, at one point, Spielberg suggested that the monkey humorously do the "Heil, Hitler" gesture. Lucas responds, "That's up to you and the trainer and the monkey." Hehehe…

They had to be laughing as they were talking about this.

So we're back at the dinner scene. The exposition about the Staff of Ra will be fed to the audience in the context of Indy possibly eating poisoned food. It'll be a bad secret agent monkey that eats the food and dies. Spielberg had a hilarious suggestion that I loved:

S—…it would be funny if, as they're talking about this and the olives are between them, you see a hairy little paw is pulling olives off the plate, coming in and out of frame. Finally the paw comes up to grab an olive and begins slipping, like palsy. You use a little mechanical paw. And then you hear a thump.

Of course, the final result was the quick "bad dates" scene. All of that thought and work for something so quick. Welcome to Hollywood.

No idea is a bad idea when you're brainstorming.

These guys were all over the place with ideas and there's nothing wrong with that. As I mentioned earlier, many of the ideas discussed, like the plane crash sequence and mine cart chase, were used in the second film. So what helped determine which sequence should be kept and thrown away?

Redundancies in concept. You already had a chase scene here, so why have another one here? Let's come up with something different. You know? That kind of thing.

At one point, when the bad guys had captured Marion, they were debating what to do next.

G—What can he chase them with? What if he jumps on a camel?

S—I love it. It's a great idea. There's never been a camel chase before.

L—Is this camel going to chase a car?

S—You know how fast a camel can run? Not only that, he can jump over vegetable carts and things. It could be a funny chase that ends in tragedy. You're laughing your head off and suddenly, "My God, she's dead."

Also:

S—We still have the big fight in the moving truck to do. And now we have a camel chase.

G—We've added another million dollars.

S—Not really. How much trouble can a camel be?

Hehehe...

Consider their approach to budget.

Keeping the film cheap was a way of testing the idea of Indiana Smith. Lucas said, "Part of it is the energy of making it reasonably low budget. It's also a test of the idea. If it's good, then we'll be okay."

Consider their approach to the ending.

G—If you follow classic dramatic plotting, that's what is going to happen. You put your biggest boom last, and you create as much tension as you possibly can.

I've also been saying this for years, what I coined, "The Big Bang Theory of Screenwriting." If you're going to have a big bang in the beginning, you sure as hell better have a bigger bang in the end.

There was a lot of discussion about the ending and ideas about how to make it bigger than the opening sequence. This involved a sub to a secret island, the ritual with the Ark, everyone getting fried, Indy saving Marion, a mine cart chase back to the sub, and somehow the entire island completely blowing up. Interesting how early concepts had Indy much more active about resolving the conflict and yet how strangely satisfying the ending is with Indy just closing his eyes.

And finally:

Consider the transcript as a whole, the sheer volume of thought, discussion, analysis, questions, and debate about the story before they ever sat down to write the script.

It's like what Billy Wilder said, "You always start with too many ideas."

Raiders looked deceptively simple and easy and fun, but the story required so much more thought than you can imagine. The good films always make everything look so easy but they never are. And I suspect that many aspiring writers fail because they jump into their stories with too few ideas, without brainstorming first, without outlining, and without really thinking through the story. Certainly not to this degree as we see in these story conferences. And so the question is, "Have you put as much thought into your story?"

Let me conclude with this anecdote from *Raider.net*:

By August 1978 Kasdan had finished his first draft and hand-delivered it to Lucas. When they met Lucas took the script, laid it aside, told Kasdan that he would read it later that night and offered him to go for lunch. During the lunch in the restaurant, Lucas offered to Kasdan to write the script for *The Empire Strikes Back*. Unfortunately, Leigh Brackett, the film's writer had passed away right after delivering her first draft and Lucas wanted someone to make revisions. "Don't you think you should read *Raiders* first?" was Kasdan's reply. "Well, I just get a feeling about people. Of course if I hate *Raiders*, I'll take back this offer," said Lucas. The next morning, Lucas called Kasdan and told him he was ecstatic about the *Raiders* script and he was very anxious for him to work on *Empire*.

EXERCISES TO INCREASE PRODUCTIVITY

I'm including this list of exercises that I use to help writing, because many of them will be of use even in the plotting process.

Make sure that your mind is clear, that you've freed yourself from stress, and that you have a "protected" time and place to write. Do anything else that you need to do in order to enter a writer's trance. This might include sitting in your favorite chair, having a cup of cocoa handy, and so on.

Many of these exercises can be done while brainstorming with other writers. Brainstorming works best in small groups—two or three writers. If you belong to a writer's group, try having frequent brainstorming sessions with them.

Once you're ready, you can begin working on your novel.

—Try cloud writing—Clear your mind and on a blank piece of paper, write down all of the images that come to mind. Circle the ones that you feel most compelled to put into a story.(This makes them look like 'clouds'.) Be aware that these images might be little bits of story that have come to you as you consider your novel over months and months.

—Draw arrows that point from each image to the next one that you might put into a following scene, so that you figure out how they are connected. Allow the images to coalesce into a story or characters.

—This exercise is surprisingly good at helping you draw scenes out of your subconscious and begin putting them on paper.

—Create your world. Make notes on your civilizations, lands, customs, and so on. Consider how your characters will grow out of this world, and what they might do to mend its wrongs—such as problems in its societies, or the effects of disasters.

—Research your world. This might include studying pictures of various lands, reading travel books, or making actual visits to an area. For example, if you have a story set in an ocean oil-drilling platform, you might actually see if you can visit one for a day.

—Consider whether to make your world a character. By this I mean, decide how your world—towns, buildings, countries—might shift or grow over the course of a story.

—Research your genre. If you want to write a great horror novel that features an alien encounter, for example, you might begin by watching the best movies dealing with this, such as Alien, Predator, and War of the Worlds, and studying the best novels written about it.

—Develop Your Characters. Do an inventory of each character's wants and needs. Ask yourself, what is each character's fear? What does each character want most in life? What is his or her secret shame? What does the character love? What motivates this character to act? What do other people say behind his or her back? Create an inventory of this character's personality traits.

—As you develop characters, try using the "Casting Director's Method" for selecting a character. Pretend that you are a casting director, looking for a character for your story. Imagine that four people show up, and all of them are wrong in some way— the wrong age, gender, look, etc. Describe them. Pretend that you interview them, and listen to what they tell you about themselves. See if one seems like a fun fit for your tale.

—While you are developing your characters, consider how to create circuitry between each pair of characters that need it. This is done by looking at how certain habits or traits tend to annoy or attract one another.

—Make sure that your cast is full—that your villain has a "captain" and minions, that you hero has a love interest, family and a sidekick, and so on. Include two or three characters that are "extras," that don't fulfill any plot role in your anticipated tale. If you don't create a full cast, it will come back to bite you very quickly.

—Do a "character interview," where you imagine that you are interviewing your characters one at a time. Ask any questions that comes to mind, and then record the answers. See how your characters change and grow as a result.

—Consider how you will create sympathy for your protagonists, or how you might distance your antagonists from your readers. What strategies will you use? Once you settle on strategies, look for incidents or dialog that need to be incorporated into scenes in order to create the desired effect.

—Now begin plotting. Look for the major "plot arcs" for you character. What does your character need to accomplish? How do other characters, or nature, block him from that goal? Look for a combination of goals—external goals, internal goals, love interests, and most importantly, look at your character's self definition. How does your character see himself? How do others see him? Plot what he wants to become.

—As you create each plot line for your character, make sure that you include your villain on your plot chart. Ask yourself over and over again, what is my villain going to do to block other characters? How will my protagonists foil each other? If you don't have a villain, then what is nature (or another character) going to do to block your protagonist? Your goal here is to have your characters get involved with one another as much as possible. They think about each other, talk about each other, and move against each other.

—Look at archetypal plot elements and at elements that might resonate with other works or life. Do you want to include such things in your novel? If so, tag your plot lines in appropriate places to remind you to include those elements.

—Look at the plotting tools in your arsenal. Ask which ones you would like to use. Plot in your arguments, reveals, timebombs, reversals, dilemmas, doubling, haunting, foreshadowing, and any other tools that strike your fancy. If there is one that you haven't thought of using, try thinking of ways that you might fit it in. In particular, look at the "Hourglass of Evil," and consider how that insight might make you want to change your outline.

—As you plot, themes will begin to arise, particularly as a protagonist must fight his or her inner demons. Think about those themes and decide if you will need to insert scenes to expound upon them. For example, let's say that you are dealing with a protagonist who suffers from greed. You might ask yourself, what scenes do I need to add, or partial scenes do I need to change, to expose this character's flaw? How will I show growth? Ultimately, how will I redeem the character?

—Set goals for your story. If there is a piece of writing that you particularly admire, consider how you might beat it. For example, let's say that you have always thought that the battle for Helm's Deep in *The Lord of the Rings* is the coolest you've ever seen. Figure out how to beat it. Or maybe you think that the prologue to *The Wheel of Time* is the most gripping you've ever seen. Figure out how to beat it. This might require you to create certain scenes that you didn't at first anticipate.

—Considering the age and sex of your protagonists, look at the emotional beats that you need for scenes. Do you need to create scenes that arouse a sense of wonder? Do you need instances of romance or mystery? As you figure out which of these emotional beats that you need to add, brainstorm ways that you might include them in your outline.

—By now, you will have filled in many pieces of your "story puzzle." You should have a good plot chart, one with the highs and lows mapped. Go through it and begin describing each scene. Tell who the viewpoint character will be, using Orson Scott Card's information from *Characters and Viewpoint* as a guide. This means that the character in the most pain will probably be your protagonist, but powerful characters of any kind might fit that bill. Describe the action that takes place in the scene, and describe the setting. Throw in dialog or lines that excite you. When you finish, you should have a long document—sixty or even a hundred pages—that acts as a map for your novel. When you've got an extended outline, you're ready to begin writing.

—Maybe you don't feel like writing at first. That happens. Often, we feel overwhelmed the immensity of the task of creating a novel. Use a writing exercise—such as the description, duality, or the argument exercise—to get things moving for the day. The chapter will usually come together pretty quickly. There are quite a few exercises that might help. For example, try looking in the dictionary for a word that you never use. Consider how it might be used in a sentence in your work. That will often get you started on a scene.

—Once the novel is started, if you get a couple of chapters in and don't feel like writing, consider whether you've made a false move. Did you end a conflict too soon? Did you have a character act in a way that feels false? If so, you might need to back up a step and edit out mistakes or make changes before you move on.

—If you just don't want to write because you feel that you've gone cold on the manuscript, then go back and re-read what you've done—maybe for the past forty pages. Make editing changes as you go. By the time that you've edited a chapter or two, you'll normally feel ready to move forward.

—Read for inspiration. Very often, reading the works of others for a limited time, say half an hour in the morning, will not only get you into the mood to write, it might inspire new ideas on how to handle your own story. Music or art will often do the same.

Learn more on how to improve your writing and enhance your stories from David Farland's other writing books.

ABOUT
DAVID FARLAND

David Farland is an award-winning, international best-selling author with over 50 novels in print. He has won the Philip K. Dick Memorial Special Award for "Best Novel in the English Language" for his science fiction novel *On My Way to Paradise*, the Whitney Award for "Best Novel of the Year" for his historical novel *In the Company of Angels*, and he has won over seven awards—including the International Book Award and the Hollywood Book Festival, Grand Prize—for his fantasy thriller *Nightingale*. He is best known, however, for his *New York Times* best-selling fantasy series *The Runelords*, which will soon be made into a graphic novel and, likely, a movie.

Farland has written for major franchises such as *Star Wars* and *The Mummy*. In the video game industry, he has been both a designer and a scripter and was the co-leader on the design team for *StarCraft: Brood War*.

As a writing instructor, Farland has mentored dozens who have gone on to staggering literary success, including such #1 *New York Times* Bestsellers as Brandon Mull (*Fablehaven*), Brandon Sanderson (*Wheel of Time*), James Dashner (*The Maze Runner*) and Stephenie Meyer (*Twilight*).

Farland judges L. Ron Hubbard's Writers of the Future, perhaps the largest worldwide writing competition for new fantasy and science fiction authors. He has worked in Hollywood greenlighting movies and doctoring scripts. He set the Guinness World Record for the largest single-author, single-book signing.

Dave is also one of the founding instructors of the Superstars Writing Seminars with bestselling authors Kevin J. Anderson, Brandon Sanderson, Rebecca Moesta, Eric Flint, and James Artimus Owen, superstarswriting.com

David Farland has been hailed as "The wizard of storytelling" and his work has been called "compelling," "engrossing," "powerful," "profound," and "ultimately life-changing."

OTHER WORDFIRE PRESS BOOKS

Be sure to check out the growing list of other great WordFire Press titles at:

wordfirepress.com

Made in the USA
Lexington, KY
16 September 2014